Korea
Kong
Japan
Philippines
N
E
S

Lobster in coconut, Bali style (see recipe page 52)

NINA FROUD

FAR EASTERN
cooking for pleasure

HAMLYN
LONDON · NEW YORK · SYDNEY · TORONTO

Published by
THE HAMLYN PUBLISHING GROUP LIMITED
LONDON · NEW YORK · SYDNEY · TORONTO
Hamlyn House, Feltham, Middlesex, England

ISBN 0 600 01318 9
Printed in Czechoslovakia by PZ, Bratislava
52026

CONTENTS

INTRODUCTION

Far Eastern cookery is such an enormous subject that one can't hope to present an exhaustive picture in a single volume. I have, therefore, tried to give as comprehensive an outline as possible, illustrated by examples of typical dishes.
The most dominating influence in Far Eastern cookery is that of China, although, as will be seen from the collection presented in this book, each country has evolved a method and style of its own which gives its food a particular character.
Although in the chapters which follow there are many original local dishes, it is inevitable that some of the dishes occur more than once. But, after all, if we study the cuisines of Europe we shall find various basic preparations such as sauces cropping up again and again.
The important thing is the new emphasis and characteristic refinements which different countries give to the same dishes.
Time and again, in small and – by certain Western standards – primitive communities, where no housewife has ever owned a refrigerator and few do their cooking on anything more elaborate than a heap of bricks housing a charcoal burner, a great deal of delicious and extremely delicate food is produced. I once enjoyed a superb meal which came from a Malaysian kitchen, where the only measuring utensils were a well-washed cigarette tin and its lid.
That cigarette tin has taught me a lot. Although a list of desirable utensils is given for most sections of this book, no one need give up the idea of preparing, say, a Chinese meal because he or she doesn't possess a wok! (*Concave iron pan illustrated above.*)

SOME KITCHEN UTENSILS

A reasonably equipped, ordinary Western kitchen should be perfectly adequate for Far Eastern cookery, but there are a few utensils which would be of advantage.

For Chinese cookery, use a good chopping block and an all-purpose cleaver, which Chinese cooks employ for a great many operations: jointing, slicing, chopping. An oval pot with a basket big enough to take a whole fish or fowl is generally used for deep frying. A wok – a concave, tempered iron pan – is useful, for it does duty as a saucepan, frying pan, deep-frier, sauté pan and braising pan. Being smooth-sided, it allows food to be turned quickly without spilling, and is ideal for frying rice. These utensils come in useful for preparing dishes of many other countries.

Lastly, if you would like to prepare and serve your own dim sum (which in Chinese means something like 'morsels to touch the heart', and, for want of something better, have in English been dubbed 'steamed dumplings') you ought to have a set of bamboo steamers. They look irresistible even before their mouthwatering contents are revealed. But, of course, ordinary aluminium steamers will do. For Japanese cooking it is desirable to have a selection of knives for cutting vegetables and slicing sashimi, a bamboo basket for draining rice, long cooking chopsticks for handling hot foods, moulds for making sushi and fish squares, a fan for rapid cooling of food, and – my special favourite – sudare, a flexible lattice mat of fine bamboo strips, which is mainly intended for rolling sushi but has a hundred other uses.

In Malaysia, in addition to a pestle and mortar, a grinding stone is used, called batu geling, which consists of a granite slab and a roller, chiefly for quick grinding of spices for curry pastes. Malaysians also use a parut, a very efficient metal grater, for coconut, ginger, and so on.

Malaysian housewives prefer deep earthenware pots called blangah, with wide mouths and wooden lids, for making curries. A well-ordered household has one for fish and one for meat curries, because the earthenware retains the flavours of the food cooked in it.

I have deliberately left out local measuring devices. The Asian cooks are particularly clever at guessing the right quantities of all ingredients. Generally, the better the cook, the more difficult it is to pin him or her down to exact amounts.

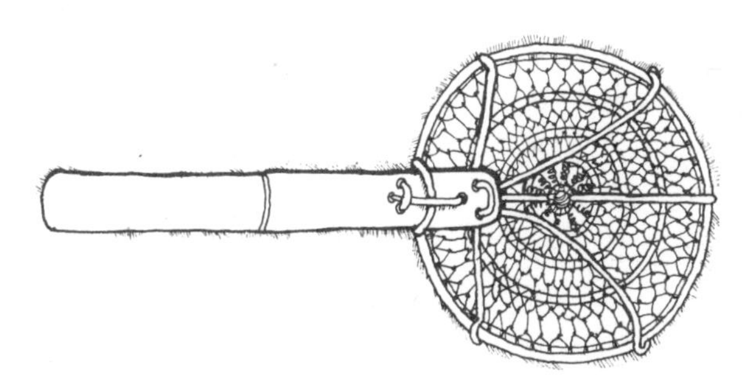

WEIGHTS AND MEASURES

English weights and measures have been used throughout. Three teaspoons equal 1 tablespoon. The average English teacup holds ¼ pint or 1 gill. The average English breakfast cup holds ½ pint or 2 gills.

When cups are mentioned in recipes they refer to a B.S.I. measuring cup which holds ½ pint or 10 fluid ounces. Three B.S.I. standard tablespoons equal approximately 2 fluid ounces.

In case it is wished to translate any of the weights and measures into their American or metric counterparts, the following notes and table give a comparison.

LIQUID MEASURE

The most important difference to be noted is that the American pint is 16 fluid ounces, as opposed to the British Imperial pint and Australian and Canadian pints which are 20 fluid ounces. The American ½-pint measuring cup is equivalent to two-fifths of a British pint. A British ½ pint (10 fluid ounces) is equal to 1¼ U.S. cups.

METRIC EQUIVALENTS

It is difficult to convert to metric measures with absolute accuracy, but 1 oz. is equal to approximately 30 grammes, 1 lb. is equal to approximately 450 grammes, 2 lb. 3 oz. to 1 kilogramme. For liquid measure, approximately 1¾ British pints (35 fluid ounces) may be regarded as equal to 1 litre; 1 demilitre is half a litre (17½ fluid ounces), and 1 decilitre is one-tenth of a litre (3½ fluid ounces).

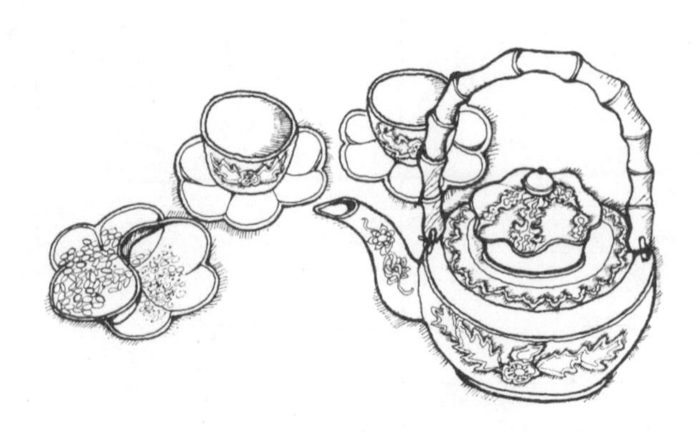

SOLID MEASURE

ENGLISH MEASUREMENTS	APPROXIMATE CONVERSION TABLE	AMERICAN MEASUREMENTS
5 oz.	Almonds, chopped	1 cup
6½ oz.	Almonds, minced	1 cup
8 oz.	Beef, uncooked	1 cup
8 oz.	Beef, minced	1½ cups
8 oz.	Chestnuts, chopped	1 cup
8 oz.	Chicken livers, minced	1 cup
8 oz.	Crab meat	1 cup
4 oz.	Flour	1 cup
6 oz.	Mushrooms, chopped	1½ cups
3–4 oz.	Mushrooms, button	1 cup
5–6 oz.	Prawns	1 cup
5½ oz.	Rice, cooked	1 cup
7 oz.	Rice, uncooked	1 cup

OVEN TEMPERATURES

DESCRIPTION	°F.	°C.	GAS MARK
very cool	225	107	¼
	250	121	½
cool	275	135	1
	300	149	2
moderate	325	163	3
	350	177	4
moderately hot	375	191	5
	400	204	6
hot	425	218	7
	450	232	8
very hot	475	252	9

Note: This table is an approximate guide only.

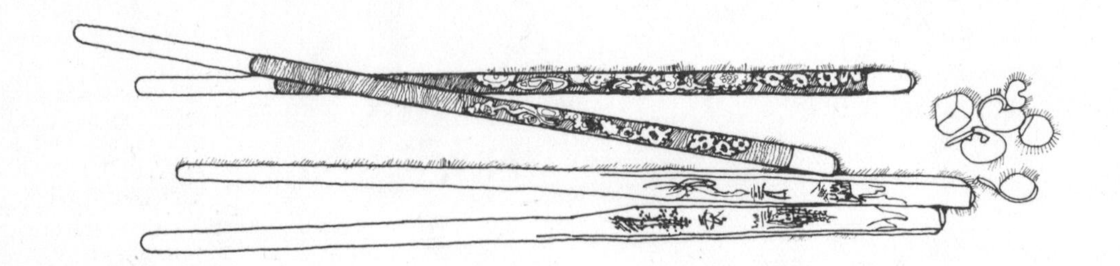

HOW TO EAT WITH CHOPSTICKS

Here are some general notes to help those who are unfamiliar with chopsticks and perhaps feel somewhat hesitant at using them.

Much of the food in the Far East is prepared in small bite-sized pieces, so it can be easily picked up with the aid of chopsticks.

For eating purposes, chopsticks are used in pairs, rather like tongs – except only one chopstick moves – the other remains stationary.

As shown in illustration 1, balance first chopstick on the base of the V formed between thumb and index finger; gently brace chopstick against upper tip of the third finger, using the second joint of the thumb to do this. This chopstick should remain stationary.

As shown in illustration 2, grip the second chopstick between thumb, index finger and middle finger. As shown in illustration 3, bend and stretch the fingers, whilst holding firm with the thumb. This moves the chopstick towards or away from the stationary chopstick, enabling morsels of food to be picked up or released as wished.

Once the action required becomes familiar, the chopsticks will not need to be gripped hard, which is the tendency of beginners. With a more relaxed movement and a little practice it will become quite natural.

Chopsticks are made of different materials, ranging from soft wood for the 'once-used, throw-away' type found in some Japanese restaurants, to priceless jade, silver and ivory pairs, regarded as heirlooms by those who own them. In between, of course, are the everyday household chopsticks made of bamboo, lacquered wood or plastic imitation ivory.

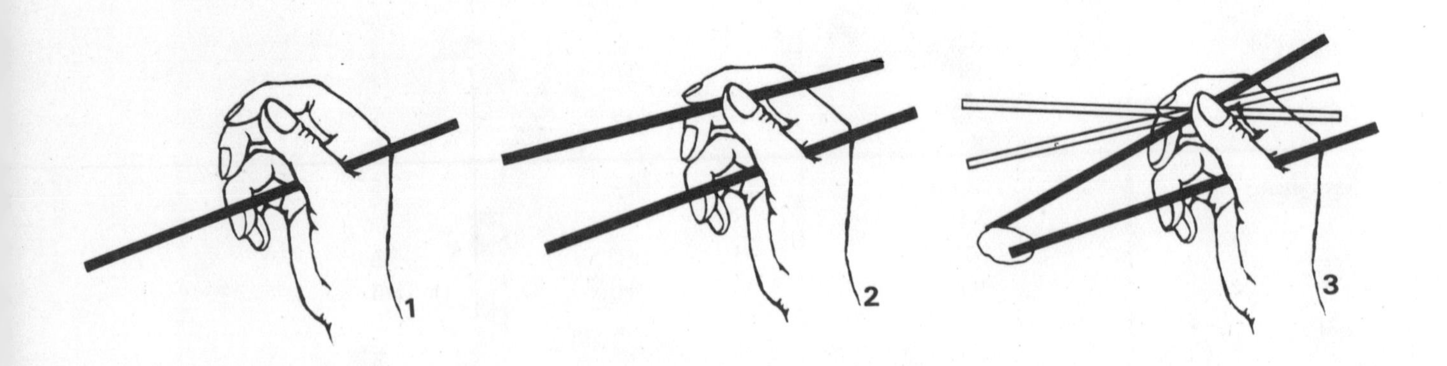

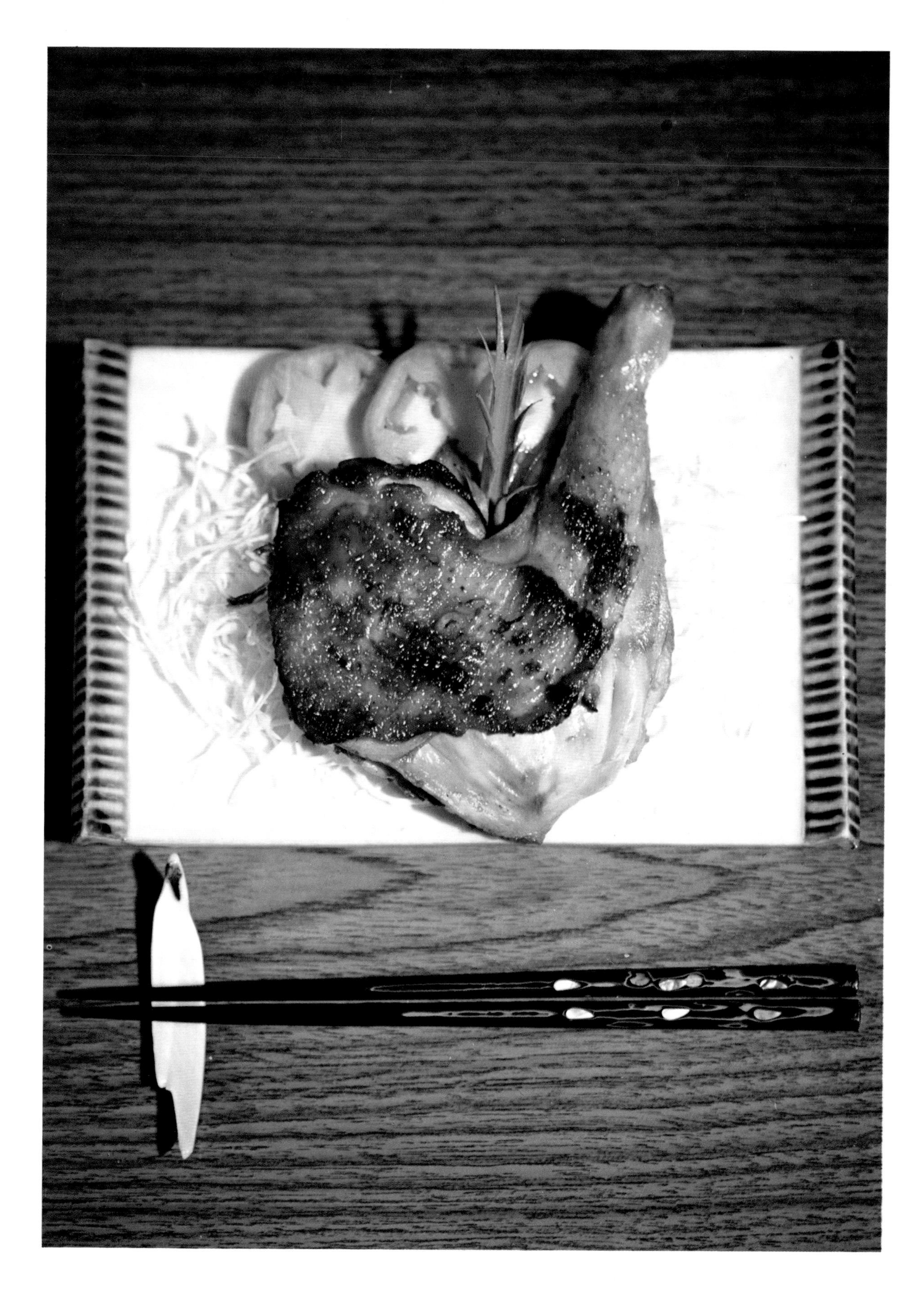

Yakitori chicken (see recipe page 34)

Sushi (see recipes pages 13–18)

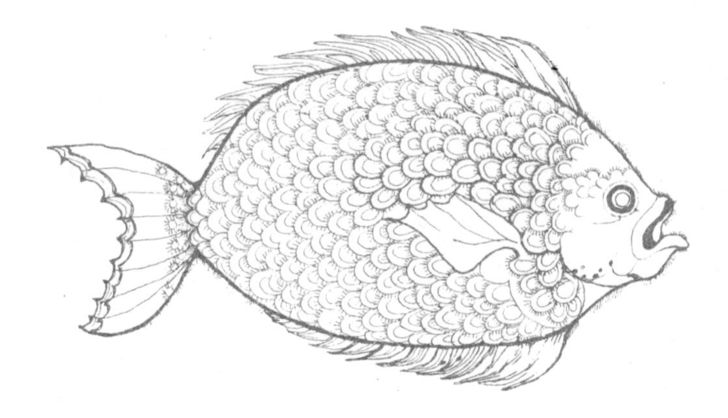

JAPAN

Many Japanese foods, ingredients and methods are derived from China and many still bear Chinese names.
Through the centuries, however, the Japanese have evolved a cuisine which is entirely their own. It is unique in many respects, perhaps most of all in its sophistication and aesthetic appeal. Japanese food is simple, but the simplicity is extremely decorative. Its main feature is freshness of raw materials and a careful balance between preserving natural flavours and judiciously enhancing them by various processes. This freshness is so highly prized that the greatest treat a Japanese host can offer his guests is the 'first of the season' of any food.
The second outstanding characteristic is the tiny size of portions, but as a guest at a Japanese meal is offered a variety of small dishes, each one a miniature work of art, no one goes away feeling hungry!

SUSHI
SNACKS

Sushi are among the most famous Japanese specialities.
These can best be described as canapes, in which rice takes the place of bread as a foundation – a sort of cold rice sandwich. People have compared them to hors d'oeuvre because of their value as appetisers, but in Japan a beautifully presented box of assorted sushi makes a complete and delicious meal. The success or failure of the dish depends entirely on the preparation of the rice. Sushi can be made with every possible ingredient: cooked or raw fish, sea bream, salmon and tunny being particularly popular; plaice, sardines, lobster, prawns, shrimps, cuttlefish, abalone, clams, eels, eggs, mushrooms, vegetables and ham are all suitable.
Sushi are so popular that they are sold at railway stations and public places just as ham sandwiches and sausage rolls are in the West. But, as everywhere else, railway food is railway food and, unless one is already a devotee, one should try the sushi in a friend's house, or a sushi-ya, a shop specialising in making sushi, where tubs of vinegared rice and all the sushi ingredients and flavourings are displayed in hygienic show cases. You choose your ingredients and the sushi are made fresh for each helping.
They are eaten with chopsticks or with the hands and, for this reason, the Japanese give each guest a small towel, not much bigger than a face cloth, rinsed in hot or cold water and wrung out, which is used as a napkin.
There are three kinds of sushi: Nigiri-zushi, rice roll covered with fish, shellfish or egg; Norimaki-zushi, rice and other ingredients rolled in nori seaweed, and Chirashi-zushi, rice mixed with various ingredients.
Nigiri-zushi are normally served a pair at a time with a small dish of sliced ginger. The Japanese drink tea with sushi and recommend taking a sip, especially when changing from one type of sushi to another, to clear the palate. Nigiri-zushi are the most difficult to make and are considered a test dish for a sushi cook. The vinegared rice is shaped into an oval cake or roll, with the ingredient chosen laid on top. The rice foundation is actually 'tailored' to the slice of fish, egg or shellfish, so that they are exactly the same size. Horseradish, finely grated, blended with a little water and reduced to a smooth paste, is used – very sparingly – with all raw fish sushi to flavour the rice, just before putting on the slice of fish. Horseradish is never used with eel or egg sushi.
Norimaki-zushi are Swiss roll type vinegared rice sandwiches, with various ingredients trapped inside in layers, encased in seasoned laver, or edible seaweed. They require six different preparations as ingredients and are often served with Nigiri-zushi.

Chirashi-zushi require no less than nine groups of ingredients which are actually mixed with vinegared rice.
In addition to the three principal types of sushi, I must mention Yushiki-zushi, or rice sandwiches wrapped in a thin egg pancake.
There are various schools of thought about the method of preparing rice for sushi. Some cooks advocate that rice should be washed three hours before cooking, others consider an hour sufficient. The seasoning varies from region to region and from one type of sushi to another. On one point, however, all authorities agree: only hard, white, polished rice is suitable for sushi.
Because the weight of rice varies considerably, quantities of rice and water have almost always been given in ½-pint measuring cups.

RICE FOR SUSHI
VINEGARED RICE

Preparation time 2 minutes plus 3 hours standing time
Cooking time 20 minutes
To make 60 sushi

You will need

8 cups rice
10 cups water
½ pint (U.S. 1¼ cups) vinegar
2 tablespoons salt
1½ tablespoons sugar
pinch monosodium glutamate (optional)

Wash rice carefully three hours before cooking, pour into a draining basket and leave. Bring water to the boil, add rice, keep boiling hard, lower heat when rice begins to bubble, simmer for 10 minutes. This should give the rice the required firm consistency. Transfer to a shallow bowl and fan to cool. Divide the rice in half. Mix one part with vinegar and 1 tablespoon salt. Mix other half with the rest of the ingredients. The two mixtures can either be used together or separately, depending on ingredients used to put on them and on how sweet or sharp you like your sushi.

Note

How much this is depends on what size cup you use – but the water must be in proportion. For a first experiment try 2 cups rice plus 2¼ cups water, 3 tablespoons vinegar, 2 teaspoons salt, 1½ teaspoons sugar, pinch monosodium glutamate.

OSAKA SUSHI RICE
VINEGARED RICE, OSAKA STYLE

Preparation time 10 minutes plus 1 hour standing time
Cooking time 20 minutes
To serve 10–12

You will need

8 cups rice
8 cups water
1½ oz. kombu seaweed
½ pint (U.S, 1¼ cups) mirin or sweet white wine
½ pint (U.S. 1¼ cups) vinegar
3 oz. sugar
4 teaspoons salt
1 teaspoon monosodium glutamate (optional)

Using above ingredients, cook and season rice as described in Tokyo Sushi Rice (see page 14).

TOKYO SUSHI RICE
VINEGARED RICE, TOKYO STYLE

Preparation time 10 minutes plus 1 hour standing time
Cooking time 20 minutes
To serve 10–12

You will need

8 cups rice
10 cups water
1½ oz. kombu seaweed
½ pint (U.S. 1¼ cups) mirin *or* sweet white wine
generous ½ pint (U.S. 1½ cups) sweet vinegar (yamabukizu)
3 tablespoons salt
1 teaspoon monosodium glutamate (optional)

Wash rice one hour before cooking and leave in a draining basket. Bring water to the boil with seaweed and wine. As soon as boiling is established, take seaweed out with a perforated spoon, put in rice, bring to the boil, simmer on a low heat for 4 minutes, then increase heat to hasten evaporation. As soon as all water disappears, turn off the heat and leave rice to stand for 5 minutes. Transfer to a shallow dish. Mix yamabukizu vinegar with salt and monosodium glutamate, quickly stir into the rice, fanning it to cool.

Note

If yamabukizu vinegar is not obtainable, use $\frac{1}{2}$ pint (U.S. $1\frac{1}{4}$ cups) ordinary vinegar, 3 tablespoons sugar, 3 teaspoons salt and a pinch monosodium glutamate.

NIGIRI-ZUSHI
RICE CANAPES

Although recipes are given for individual types of Nigiri-zushi, it is usual to serve sushi as an artistically arranged assortment. As many as a dozen varieties may be packed in one box or dish, using their shape and colours to the greatest pictorial advantage.

PRAWN NIGIRI-ZUSHI
PRAWN AND RICE CANAPES

(Illustrated in black and white on the right)

Preparation time 40 minutes
Cooking time 5–10 minutes
Makes 24 sushi

You will need

24 prawns, cleaned and peeled
12 oz. sushi rice (see page 14)
4 teaspoons horseradish
soya sauce

The prawns can be used raw or cooked. (To cook, before peeling boil in lightly salted water until they turn red.)
Use whichever of the previous rice recipes you prefer. Moisten hands with water, take a spoonful of the vinegared rice in your left hand and form into a shape to fit one prawn. Brush on a little horseradish with the index finger of your right hand. Wipe finger and take up a prawn in your right hand. Place prawn on top of horseradish and press with the fingers to give the sushi a regular form. Put on dish. Rinse or wipe your hands and proceed to make the rest of the sushi in the same way. Serve with a dish of soya sauce in which you dip each mouthful.

Sushi and sashami (see recipes pages 13–18 and 22–23)

NIGIRI-ZUSHI WITH EGGS
OMELETTE RICE CANAPES

Preparation time 15 minutes
Cooking time 5 minutes
Makes 8 sushi

You will need

1 small sole fillet
2 eggs
$\frac{1}{2}$ teaspoon soya sauce
small pinch salt
1 tablespoon sugar (optional)
4 oz. sushi rice (see page 14)

Pound fish in a mortar to reduce to a smooth paste. Whisk eggs with soya sauce, salt and sugar. Add fish and blend well. Grease a square omelette pan very lightly, fry the eggs and sole mixture. Cut into eight rectangles, each 1 inch wide and 2 inches long, and use with the rice to make Nigiri-zushi as described on page 15, substituting the omelette rectangles for the prawns. Do not use horseradish.

NORIMAKI-ZUSHI
RICE WHEELS

Norimaki-zushi by tradition requires six layers of various ingredients, each prepared separately before rolling.

Preparation time	About 30 minutes plus 30 minutes standing time
Cooking time	25–30 minutes
To serve	4

You will need

four 1½-oz. dried gourd shavings
½ pint (U.S. 1¼ cups) dashi (see page 24)
1½ teaspoons salt
3 tablespoons soya sauce
3 oz. sugar
4 large dried mushrooms
4 oz. spinach
4 eggs
4 tablespoons sake
4 oz. plaice fillets
2 oz. peeled prawns
few drops cochineal
4 oz. salmon (or other red-fleshed fish)
5 teaspoons mirin *or* sweet white wine
sushi rice (see page 14)
7 sheets nori seaweed (seasoned laver)

Soak the gourd shavings in salted water for 30 minutes, rinse in fresh water, boil in dashi seasoned with ½ teaspoon salt, 2 tablespoons soya sauce and 1 oz. sugar. Cook until tender, then remove but keep the liquid. Meanwhile, soak mushrooms in lukewarm water for 15 minutes to soften, remove and discard stems and cut into strips.
Put 4 tablespoons of liquid left over from cooking gourd shavings into a pan, add ½ tablespoon sugar and the remaining soya sauce and cook the mushrooms in this mixture.
Wash spinach, boil lightly in salted water for 2–3 minutes and drain. Beat 2 eggs with ½ teaspoon salt, 1½ tablespoons sugar and 1½ tablespoons sake, put in a frying pan, cook quickly, add spinach and mix well. Spread egg and spinach mixture on the plaice fillets (steamed lightly, if you can't bear the thought of eating them raw), and cut lengthways into strips ¼ inch wide. Beat remaining 2 eggs. Pound prawns in a mortar, add beaten eggs and gradually stir in remaining sake, season with ¼ teaspoon salt, add 1½ tablespoons sugar and a dash of cochineal. Blend well and fry quickly in lightly greased square shaped pan. Cut into long strips. Boil the salmon (canned salmon may be used and needs no cooking), pound in a mortar, season with ¼ teaspoon salt, add ½ tablespoon sugar and wine. Scramble quickly over low heat, stirring all the time. You should now have six preparations: (1) gourd, (2) mushrooms, (3) strips of plaice with egg and spinach, (4) fried prawn and egg, (5) salmon and (6) sushi rice. We now come to the main operation of rolling Norimaki-zushi and simultaneously wrapping them in seaweed. Hold seaweed over direct heat to crisp it. Lay a sheet of it on a sudare (bamboo mat). Spread some of the sushi rice on this in a thick, even layer. Let the rice come up to the edge of the seaweed on the sides, but leave about ¾ inch uncovered seaweed at top and bottom ends to allow for the essential overlap.
Put some of each preparation (this will form the centre of the Norimaki-zushi) on top of the rice, in a horizontal row, starting with a line of gourd along the bottom, then a line of mushrooms above it, and so on. Roll up the ingredients, using the sudare, being careful to ensure that the seaweed forms a tight casing around them. The secret is to make a good tight roll. Remove sudare, cut the roll with

Fresh dwarf French beans (see recipe page 18)

a sharp knife into 8–9 pieces. Repeat with the rest of the seaweed and ingredients. Lay the Norimaki-zushi in such a way as to display their multi-coloured filling and serve with Nigiri-zushi (see page 15).

Note

Norimaki-zushi can be served on a separate dish, arranged in little groups of two or three to resemble flowers, with a lightly cooked runner bean forming the stem of each flower.

YUSHIKI-ZUSHI
RICE-STUFFED PANCAKES

Preparation time	13 hours – including standing time (only 1 hour if gourd is used instead of seaweed)
Cooking time	1 hour 10 minutes
To serve	4

You will need

10-inch square piece of kombu seaweed *or* four 10-inch strips dried gourd
vinegar
2 cups rice
2 dried mushrooms
4 tablespoons dashi (see page 24)
5 teaspoons soya sauce
5 teaspoons sake *or* sherry
1 tablespoon mirin *or* sweet white wine
2 teaspoons sugar
½ oz. dried gourd
salt
2 oz. bamboo shoots
2 young carrots
2 oz. haddock fillet
monosodium glutamate (optional)
few drops cochineal
4 large shrimps
1–2 tablespoons shelled peas
4 eggs
1 teaspoon cornflour
oil
4 pepper sprouts
½ oz. red pickled ginger

If you can get kombu seaweed, cover with vinegar and leave to soak overnight to soften. Next day cut into thin, string-like strips and use for tying the Yushiki-zushi. (If kombu is not available, use dried gourd which does not need to be soaked overnight.)

Cook rice as described in the recipe for Osaka Sushi Rice (see page 14) and add prescribed seasoning and flavourings.

Soak mushrooms in warm water for 15 minutes, remove and discard stems, cook in a mixture of 2 tablespoons dashi, the soya sauce, sake, wine and 1½ teaspoons sugar. Simmer until tender, take out of the sauce with a perforated spoon and cut into narrow strips. Reserve sauce. Wash gourd (including the 10-inch strips, if using) thoroughly in cold water, rub with salt, parboil in water until softened, and drain. Add 2 tablespoons dashi, pinch of salt and ½ teaspoon sugar to the liquid in which mushrooms were cooked, put in gourd, simmer until thoroughly impregnated with the sauce, drain and keep the liquid. Cut the gourds into ¾-inch strips reserving the four 10-inch ones for tying up the sushi, if you have no kombu seaweed.

Cut bamboo shoots and carrots into ¾-inch strips and simmer until tender in the sauce left over from cooking gourd strips.

Boil haddock fillet in a little salted water – enough to cover – until cocktail stick penetrates flesh easily. Remove, drain, mince, season with pinch of salt, sugar and monosodium glutamate to taste. Add a minute amount of cochineal colouring, return to heat and cook gently, stirring all the time, until all liquid has been completely reduced.

Clean shrimps, de-vein, insert a cocktail stick into back of each shrimp to keep it straight, boil in salted water until tender, drain, shell except for the tail tip, slit underside without cutting right through, open out and flatten gently. This makes them look larger than they are.

Boil peas in a little salted water until tender. Avoid overcooking. (The frozen variety will need 2 minutes. It is important to preserve their green colour.)

Mix rice with mushrooms, ¾-inch strips of gourd, bamboo shoots and carrots, and divide the mixture into four portions.

Taking one egg at a time, stir (do not whisk) with a pinch of salt and monosodium glutamate and a quarter of the cornflour diluted in 1 teaspoon water. Blend well and strain. Fry in a big, lightly oiled pan to make thin pancake. Cook on one side only.

Lay this omelette pancake, cooked side down, on a board, put a portion of rice on it, a quarter of the haddock on the rice, top with a shrimp, stud with a quarter of the peas, decorate with a pepper sprout, wrap up, folding in the sides of the egg pancake neatly, tie with kombu seaweed (or gourd 'string'), making a pretty bow. Make the remaining three in the same way. It is better to make these sushi one at a time, as the pancake is cooked, while it is at its most pliable. Garnish with red pickled ginger. The Yushiki-zushi make a very attractive picture decorated with a small spray of young bamboo leaves.

CHIRASHI-ZUSHI
RICE VOLCANOES

This is the third most popular sushi. It is based on vinegared rice, but it has three features which distinguish it from all other sushi: it requires nine different preparations, is neither moulded nor rolled but arranged on plates with the more colourful ingredients disposed in separate groups in a pleasing visual manner, and it can be served cold or warm. In Japan Chirashi-zushi is considered highly suitable for a main course party dish.

Preparation time	30 minutes plus 1 hour standing time
Cooking time	48–50 minutes
To serve	4

You will need

3½ cups polished rice
3¾ cups water
salt
sugar
vinegar
2 eggs
½ pint (U.S. 1¼ cups) dashi (see page 24)
oil
1½ oz. green beans
1½ oz. salmon (canned or poached)
1 teaspoon sake *or* sherry
3 oz. white-fleshed fish
½ oz. dried mushrooms
1½ oz. dried gourd shavings
½ oz. bean curd
4 tablespoons soya sauce
2 young carrots
3 oz. lotus root or chestnuts
½ oz. red pickled ginger

Prepare and boil rice in water (see Tokyo Sushi Rice page 14). Season with 2 teaspoons salt, 2 tablespoons sugar and 3 tablespoons vinegar. Mix well. Beat eggs with 1½ teaspoons dashi, small pinch of salt and ¼ teaspoon sugar. Grease a square frying pan lightly with the oil and fry very thin, pancake-like omelettes. Cut in strips.
Cook the beans for a few minutes in boiling water – do not overcook. Season with ¼ teaspoon salt and ½ teaspoon sugar and mix.
Flake the salmon, mash in a bowl, stand bowl in a pan of boiling water, add sake, small pinch salt and ½ teaspoon sugar, and steam for a few minutes to amalgamate mixture.
Rub the white fleshed fish (hake, halibut, cod and other white-fleshed fish are suitable for this dish – fresh haddock is particularly good), with a teaspoon of salt, simmer in a little water until soft, strain and mash.
Soak, discard stems and shred mushrooms; prepare gourd as described for Norimaki-zushi (page 16). Rinse the bean curd, press out excess liquid, put in a bowl, add mushrooms and gourd, moisten with 3 tablespoons dashi, season with soya sauce and add 4 tablespoons sugar. Mix well. Slice or shred carrots, add 3 tablespoons dashi, ¼ teaspoon salt and ½ teaspoon sugar, boil gently until soft, stirring to mix well. Peel and chop lotus root (if chestnuts are used, they should be shelled and peeled), simmer gently in enough dashi to cover, with 1 tablespoon vinegar, 1 tablespoon sugar and ¼ teaspoon salt, until they turn white. This should only take a couple of minutes.
Cut ginger into thinnest possible slivers, or shred it. Mix rice with white fish, carrots, gourd shavings and mushrooms. Divide among 4 individual dishes, heaping it to a point. Arrange the rest of the prepared ingredients on top in a decorative manner, reserving the fine strips of red ginger for the pinnacle. Serve.
The above is a fairly classical Chirashi-zushi, but the ingredients may be varied, provided they add up to the right number. In Japan kamaboko fish paste, bamboo shoots, dried sardines, prawns and shrimps are frequently included.

HOW TO COOK RICE THE JAPANESE WAY

Needless to say, the proportion of water to rice will differ according to the consistency desired. The Japanese have a special utensil for cooking rice, called a kama. The rice is cooked, as is much of the food, on a charcoal burning stove, or hibachi. With gas and electric cookers, a thick bottomed saucepan with a lid, or a double saucepan, is best.
There are two popular Japanese methods of boiling rice, both of which produce successful results, so it is a matter for experiment to see which you prefer. Allow 5 cups of water to 4 cups of rice – this will be enough for about 8 servings.
An hour before cooking, wash the rice free of all grit and impurities until the water runs clear, and leave in a draining basket. Pour it into a deep saucepan, add water and proceed as follows:

METHOD 1

Cover the pan with a lid and bring to the boil quickly. Reduce to the lowest possible heat and simmer for 3 minutes. Bring to the boil again and reduce the heat as the water evaporates. There should be no water left at the end of 18–20 minutes. Turn the heat to full for a moment (no longer than a couple of seconds) and remove from heat. Allow to stand for 6–7 minutes and serve.

METHOD 2

Cover the pan with a lid and bring to the boil quickly. Reduce the heat, simmer for 10 minutes, then reduce heat to its lowest and simmer for another 10 minutes. Turn off the heat completely but leave the pan to stand for a further 10 minutes before removing the cover.

Whichever method you choose, remember never to take the lid off the pan while the rice is cooking, because the loss of steam affects the cooking process.

It is possible to check whether any water remains by feeling the knob of the saucepan lid. The bubbling of the water causes vibration, so if you cannot feel any 'bubbling' the water has gone. The rice is cooked when all the water has been absorbed.

It is important to let the rice 'rest' for about 10 minutes after cooking, without removing the lid. This prevents the rice becoming sticky, and gives it an attractive, fluffy appearance.

MESHIMONO
RICE DISHES

SWEET AND SOUR PRAWNS

(Illustrated in black and white below)

Preparation time 20 minutes plus 2 hours standing time
Cooking time 5 minutes
To serve 6

You will need

12 prawns
$1\frac{1}{2}$ pints (U.S. $3\frac{3}{4}$ cups) water
2 teaspoons salt
2 teaspoons sugar
2 teaspoons vinegar
pinch monosodium glutamate (optional)

This recipe is equally suitable for shrimps. It can also be used for lobster and crayfish, but these have to be cut in thin slices.

Wash prawns and boil in the water seasoned with teaspoon salt. Shell, leaving tail tips on, de-vein, put in a wide bowl. Mix remaining ingredients, pour over prawns, leave to steep in marinade for 2 hours, and serve with rice.

Note

Frozen prawns or scampi may be used for this dish. In which case allow to thaw before putting into the marinade.

Sweet and sour prawns

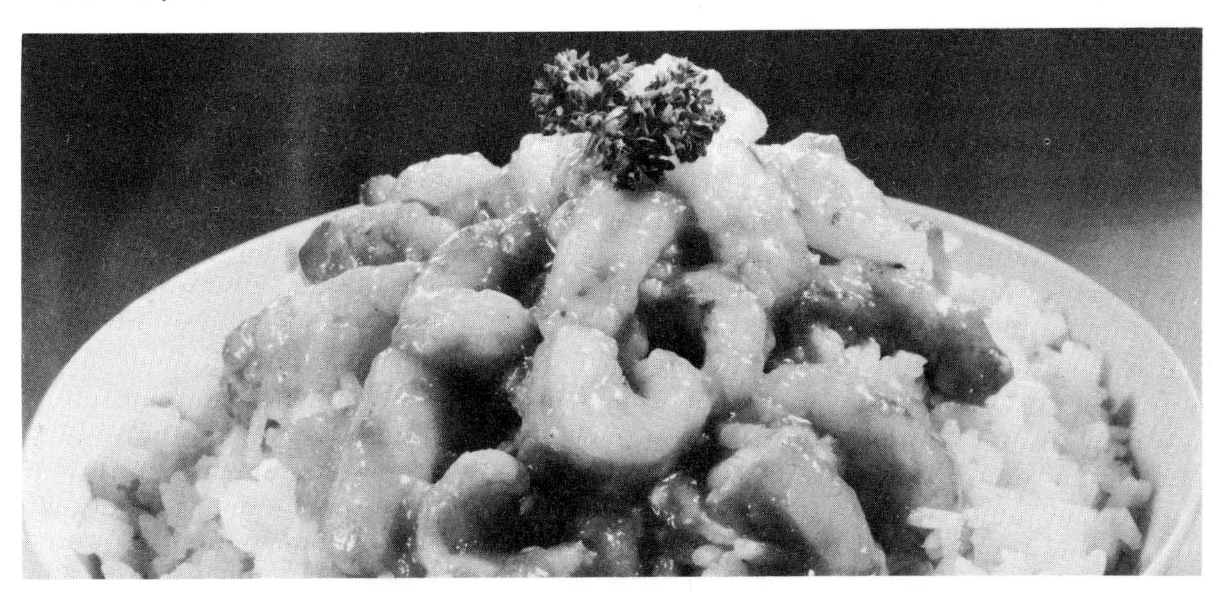

Deep-fried prawns on rice

Grilled eels on rice

PRAWN TENDON
DEEP-FRIED PRAWNS ON RICE
(Illustrated in black and white above)

Preparation time 3 minutes
Cooking time 6 minutes
To serve 4

You will need

oil for deep frying
1 lb. prawns
tempura batter (see page 32)
12 oz. hot, cooked rice
little grated daikon radish
tempura sauce (see page 33)
pinch grated ginger (optional)

Heat the oil for deep frying. Dip prawns in the batter. Deep-fry until crisp and golden, remove and drain quickly. Arrange on a mound of steaming rice.
Add the radish to the hot tempura sauce and pour over the prawns, or serve separately. Sprinkle with ginger if liked, and serve at once.

UNAGI DOMBURI
GRILLED EELS ON RICE
(Illustrated in black and white above)

Preparation time 5 minutes
Cooking time 7 minutes
To serve 4

You will need

1 lb. grilled eels (see Unagi No Kabayaki, page 35)
generous $\frac{1}{4}$ pint (U.S. $\frac{3}{4}$ cup) dashi (see page 24)
4 tablespoons mirin *or* sweet white wine
3 tablespoons soya sauce
1 lb. freshly cooked rice

Keep grilled eels hot. Meanwhile, boil eels' heads and bones in dashi for 5 minutes to flavour and reduce stock. Strain, discard heads and bones and stir in the wine and soya sauce. Reheat to boiling point and remove from the heat. Arrange steaming hot rice in individual bowls, put eels on top, pour sauce over them, cover and serve at once.

ZENSAI
HORS D'OEUVRE

Japanese zensai are similar to European hors d'oeuvre. The main difference between zensai and hors d'oeuvre is that the former, although often cooked, is almost invariably served cold and in much smaller quantities and includes sweet as well as savoury dishes.
All the specialities given in this section can be served separately, or in any combination which pleases the eye. On a special occasion in a Japanese home it is not unusual to have up to a dozen zensai, all served on the same platter.
In the case of Hakata and Chicken Oharame zensai, certain rules should be observed. Good manners decree that, if these two zensai are served together, the dish must be so placed that the Hakata is away from, and the Oharame towards, the guest to whom it is offered.
The following popular Japanese hors d'oeuvre are exported and require no preparation:

SALMON ROE

Available in small jars. Looks like red caviar. Ready to serve without any additional seasoning.

SWEET CHESTNUTS

These are available in cans, ready to serve. Allow 3 chestnuts per portion.

SWEET BOILED BEANS

These are available in cans. Ready to serve.

HAKATA
TOMATO AND EGG SANDWICH

Preparation time 20 minutes
Cooking time 5 minutes
To serve 6

You will need

2 large tomatoes
2 eggs
pinch salt
2 teaspoons sugar
pinch monosodium glutamate (optional)
1 tablespoon cooked peas
6 slices sandwich bread

Dip tomatoes into boiling water for a moment to loosen skins, peel and cut into ¼-inch slices. Beat eggs, add salt, sugar and monosodium glutamate. Heat in a pan and scramble until it becomes a paste-like consistency. Remove from heat and add peas.
Spread one slice of bread with half the egg and pea mixture; cover with another slice of bread, and place half the tomato slices on top. Finish with a third slice of bread, to form a doubledecker sandwich. Make a second sandwich with remaining bread, tomato and egg. Wrap in a damp napkin and put a heavy weight on top.
To serve: Unwrap the sandwiches, trim off edges and cut into small, dainty pieces.

TAZUNA ZUSHI
CHICKEN AND MUSHROOM SQUARES

Preparation time 15 minutes plus 15 minutes standing time
Cooking time 25 minutes
Oven temperature 191°C., 375°F., Gas Mark 5
To serve 6

You will need

3 dried mushrooms
1 oz. or 2 tablespoons bamboo shoots
2–3 spring onions
12 oz. uncooked chicken, minced
1½ tablespoons soya sauce
1½ tablespoons sake *or* sherry
pinch salt
1 teaspoon sugar
pinch monosodium glutamate (optional)
1 egg
1½ teaspoons poppy seeds

Soak mushrooms in cold water for 15 minutes; remove and discard stalks.
Turn on the oven at temperature given above. Mince the mushrooms, bamboo shoots and spring onions and mix with the chicken. Blend well, and season with soya sauce, sake or sherry, salt, sugar and monosodium glutamate. Stir in the egg. Shape into a square ¾ inch thick, place on a baking sheet and sprinkle with poppy seeds. Bake in the preheated oven until chicken is cooked – about 25 minutes.
Leave to cool, cut into 12 equal pieces and serve in dainty individual bowls, allowing 2 pieces per person.
Serve a dish of soya sauce for dipping the squares, should anyone require additional seasoning at the table.

CHICKEN AND LEMON SANDWICHES

Preparation time 5 minutes plus 1 hour 15 minutes marinating time
Cooking time 5–10 minutes
To serve 4

You will need

12 oz. boned breast of chicken
2 tablespoons soya sauce
3 tablespoons mirin *or* sweet white wine
1 tablespoon oil
2 lemons, sliced

Cut chicken into $\frac{1}{4}$-inch slices.
Mix sauce and wine and marinate the chicken in it for 45 minutes–1 hour. Drain.
Heat oil in a pan, and fry chicken slices quickly. After frying, soak in the marinade once again for 15 minutes and repeat the frying. Sandwich each slice of chicken between two slices of lemon and serve.

CHICKEN OHARAME
CHICKEN BUNDLES

Preparation time 10 minutes plus 1 hour standing time
Cooking time 5–10 minutes
To serve 6

You will need

6 oz. uncooked chicken meat
1 tablespoon soya sauce
1 tablespoon sake *or* sherry
$\frac{1}{2}$ sheet nori seaweed
1 egg white
oil for frying

Remove any skin from the chicken and cut the meat into strips each 2 inches long and $\frac{1}{4}$ inch thick. Sprinkle with soya sauce and sake and leave to marinate for 1 hour.
Cut seaweed into $\frac{1}{2}$-inch strips. Take 4–5 chicken strips at a time and make into bundles, securing round the middle with a band of seaweed, dipped in egg white to make it stick.
Fry in a very little oil, drain on greaseproof paper and serve, allowing 3–4 small bundles per portion.

SASHIMI
RAW FISH HORS D'OEUVRE

(Illustrated in colour on front cover and in black and white on page 15)

This is a great Japanese speciality, one which is considered an exquisite delicacy and consists mainly of slices of uncooked firm-fleshed fish and shell-fish, but chicken can also be used. To render it more digestible, and to add flavour, it is usually accompanied by grated wasabi (horseradish) and invariably with soya sauce. Udo, a type of herb, is a popular garnish for raw fish, and so are finely sliced or shredded raw vegetables, parsley, lettuce and cress.
To prepare, scale the fish and remove head, tail and fins. Clean well and discard entrails. Wash thoroughly and leave to soak in cold water. Bone the fish and skin the fillets.
To serve, cut the fillets with a very sharp knife, at an angle of 30 degrees, into slices $1\frac{1}{2}$ inches wide and $\frac{1}{2}$ inch thick. Choose a long, narrow dish and arrange the slices, overlapping, in the shape of a fish. Garnish and decorate to resemble, say, a bream swimming among the reeds.
Alternatively, a firm-fleshed fish can be cut into dice. Thin-fleshed fish is normally shaved off in the thinnest possible slices. Long fish should be cut into chunks of manageable size then, on a slant, into narrow, thin slices.
Lobsters, prawns, crayfish and other crustaceans undergo a different treatment in preparation for sashimi. To ensure complete freshness, only live crustaceans are used. They are killed quickly and, according to Japanese cooks, painlessly, by stabbing them with a knife in the soft part of the belly. After this, shell at once, wash the flesh with great care and continue to wash in cold running water until it stiffens. Dry on a cloth, and the meat is ready for use.

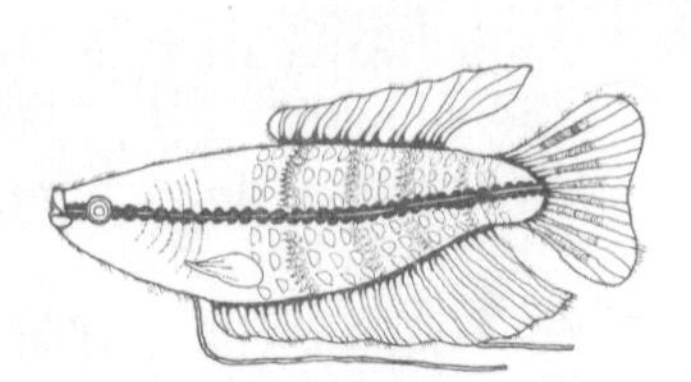

SEA BREAM SASHIMI
SEA BREAM SLICES

Preparation time 20 minutes
To serve 4

You will need

1 lb. sea bream
1 bunch watercress
2 teaspoons grated horseradish
4 tablespoons soya sauce

Prepare and slice the fish as described on page 22. Arrange on a dish in the shape of a bream, decorate with watercress to portray the fish as seen through a growth of seaweed.
Mix horseradish with sauce and serve separately. This is used for dipping the sashimi slices.

TUNNY SASHIMI
SLICED TUNNY FILLETS

Preparation time 20 minutes
To serve 4

You will need

1 lb. tunny fillets
sprigs of parsley
2 teaspoons grated ginger
4 tablespoons soya sauce

Prepare and slice the fish as described on page 22. Arrange as in recipe for Sea Bream Sashimi, using parsley for 'seaweed' and serving mixed ginger and soya sauce as an accompaniment.

Japanese always use fish straight from the sea

SUIMONO
CLEAR SOUPS

DASHI

The Japanese use dashi as the basis for stocks, soups, sauces and dressings. It is very easy to make and the ingredients are available in shops specialising in oriental produce. The two vital ingredients are kombu seaweed and bonito (tunny fish) fillets cut into shavings. In an emergency a light, strained fish stock may be used.

Cooking time 5 minutes

You will need

¼ oz. kombu seaweed
1¾ pints (U.S. 4¼ cups) water
1¼ oz. bonito shavings
¼ teaspoon monosodium glutamate (optional)

Put kombu seaweed in a pan with water and heat. Remove from the heat as soon as it boils. Add bonito, reheat, and remove from heat at the first sign of boiling. Season with monosodium glutamate, if liked. Allow to stand for 10 minutes, strain and use as required.

TORI-NO-MIZUDAKI
CHICKEN SOUP

Preparation time 15 minutes
Cooking time 1 hour 5 minutes – 1 hour 10 minutes
To serve 4

You will need

3½-lb. chicken, jointed
5 pints (U.S. 12½ cups) water
1–2 leeks, sliced
1 tablespoon salt
juice of 1 lemon
3 tablespoons soya sauce

Bone the chicken joints and put meat and bones in a pan of water. Bring to the boil, skim and simmer until the meat is tender. Carefully remove all bones. Cut meat into large dice, add leeks, put back in the pan and reheat.
Mix salt, lemon juice and soya sauce and stir the mixture into the soup. Simmer for a few minutes, just long enough for the leeks to cook through, and serve in individual, covered bowls. A small dish of very fine, dry salt is often served. The guests dip pieces of chicken into it if they want more seasoning.
Note
In Japan, bitter orange juice is often used instead of lemon juice for this soup.

CHICKEN BONE STOCK

Cooking time 45 minutes

You will need

1 lb. chicken bones
2 small pieces ginger, crushed
2 spring onions
3½ pints (U.S. 9 cups) water

Put all the ingredients in a pan. Bring to the boil, skim from time to time to remove scum and excess fat, and simmer gently to reduce the liquid by half. Strain. Use this stock for soup.

TREFOIL AND TRIANGULAR EGG SOUP

Preparation time 15 minutes plus about 15 minutes standing time
Cooking time 7 minutes
To serve 4

You will need

4 sheets paper
4 eggs
12 trefoils (Japanese green vegetable with 3 leaves)
4 Japanese pepper sprouts*
1¾ pints (U.S. 4¼ cups) seasoned clear stock

Fold 1 sheet of paper in half, short end to short end, then in half the other way. Holding three layers together, separate one and break an egg into the pointed pocket so formed. Repeat with the other sheets of paper and eggs. Stand the 4 pockets, points downward, in a pan of boiling water. Cook for 7 minutes, then take them out of the water, but do not remove the eggs from the paper. Chill, remove paper, and you have four triangular cooked eggs. Tie the trefoils in bundles of three and trim to uni-

form length. Dip into boiling salted water, then into cold water, and drain.
Trim eggs to remove any untidy edges, put one in each individual soup bowl, and decorate with trefoils and pepper sprouts. Cover with hot, seasoned, clear stock, cover the bowl with its lid, and serve. This soup looks most attractive in black-lined lacquer bowls.

**Note*

If Japanese pepper sprouts are not available, use a small piece of lemon peel cut into a suitable decorative shape. Watercress can be stripped to resemble trefoil.

CUSTARD AND SPINACH SOUP

Preparation time 15 minutes plus about 15 minutes standing time
Cooking time 40–45 minutes
To serve 4

You will need

8 eggs
$\frac{3}{4}$ pint (U.S. 2 cups) dashi (see page 24)
$1\frac{1}{2}$ teaspoons soya sauce
pinch sugar
$\frac{1}{2}$ teaspoon monosodium glutamate (optional)
4 oz. spinach
salt
$1\frac{1}{2}$ pints (U.S. $3\frac{3}{4}$ cups) seasoned, clear stock
grapefruit peel

Beat the eggs, add the dashi, sauce, sugar and monosodium glutamate. Whisk, strain and pour into a shallow mould (square for preference). Steam over a pan of hot water or in a bain-marie for 30–35 minutes on the lowest possible heat. Cool and turn out of the mould, cut into squares (each 2 inches across) and chill.
Cook spinach, uncovered, in slightly salted boiling water for 3–4 minutes, rinse with cold water, drain and cut into strips. This spinach is used for decorating the custard squares and should fit neatly in the middle, leaving the edges free, so the strips should be cut about $\frac{1}{2}$ inch shorter than the width of the custard square. Put 1 custard square into each bowl and lay a spinach strip on top. Heat the stock and carefully fill the bowls without dislodging the spinach.
Cut a small rosette of thinly sliced grapefruit peel, put it as a decoration in the middle of the spinach strip. Cover the bowls with lids and serve.

KAKITAMAJIRU SUIMONO
EGG DROP SOUP

Preparation time 10 minutes
Cooking time 15 minutes
To serve 4

You will need

$1\frac{3}{4}$ pints (U.S. $4\frac{1}{4}$ cups) dashi (see page 24)
2 teaspoons cornflour
$1\frac{1}{2}$ teaspoons salt
1 teaspoon sake *or* sherry
2 teaspoons soya sauce
2 eggs
1 piece ginger, thinly sliced
1 sprig parsley

Bring dashi to the boil. Blend together cornflour, salt, sake and soya sauce. Add to dashi and simmer for a few minutes.
Beat eggs to a froth and, using a perforated spoon, float pieces on to the surface of the soup, which should be kept simmering on very low heat. Do not pour in the egg mixture, as it will sink below the surface.
Pour soup into individual bowls, add a slice of ginger to each, decorate with a small 'posy' of parsley, cover with a lid, and serve.

Fresh spinach

MATSUTAKE SUIMONO
TREE MUSHROOM SOUP

Preparation time 15 minutes plus 30 minutes standing time
Cooking time 13 minutes
To serve 4

You will need

8 oz. skinned, boned uncooked chicken
salt
cornflour
2 matsutake mushrooms
$1\frac{3}{4}$ pints (U.S. $4\frac{1}{4}$ cups) stock
lemon peel

Cut the chicken into 8 pieces. Sprinkle with salt and leave to stand for 30 minutes. Dip in cornflour to coat thoroughly, then put into boiling salted water and simmer until tender. Drain and keep hot.
Cut off mushroom stems and discard, wash and cut mushrooms into quarters. Boil the mushrooms slowly in stock for 3 minutes, drain, but keep the stock. Put portions of chicken and mushrooms in individual bowls, add a piece of lemon peel and pour in the hot stock. Cover with a lid and serve.
Note
Sometimes canned matsutake (tree mushrooms) are available in delicatessen and need no cooking.

SUMASHI-SHIRU AND MISO-SHIRU
THICK SOUPS

There is a wide variety of Japanese thick soups, made of fish, meat, shellfish and vegetables. The same flavourings and seasonings are used for thick as for clear soups. Sumashi-shiru are often described on Japanese menus, intended for Western restaurant clients, as 'stew soups'.
Miso-shiru require one essential ingredient, miso, which is fermented bean paste used as a liaison for thickening. Dashi is used as stock for both types of thick soup.
Several varieties of miso can be bought, such as white miso, brown miso and chu-miso. The type required for each recipe is indicated in the list of ingredients.
To thicken the soup, miso paste is dissolved in a little stock, poured into the soup, stirred in and brought to the boil. As with all liaisons, the soup should not be allowed to boil after the miso has been added.
Many miso soups are eaten at breakfast. These are principally light soups, based on dashi and garnished with seaweed, shellfish, vegetables, and so on. Miso soups for other meals (mainly eaten in the evening) are made with meats of various kinds, poultry or fish.
Soya bean curd, tofu, is also widely used for these soups.

PRAWN MISO SOUP

Preparation time 5 minutes
Cooking time 8–9 minutes
To serve 4

You will need

6 oz. peeled prawns
4 oz. chu-miso
$1\frac{1}{2}$ pints (U.S. $3\frac{3}{4}$ cups) dashi (see page 24)
6 oz. bean curd, diced
powdered ginger

Chop the prawns, rub through a sieve with 1 teaspoon miso, and blend well.
To make the soup, bring the dashi to the boil, add the prawns, bean curd and the rest of the miso. Simmer 3–4 minutes, then strain.
Put a helping of prawn forcemeat and bean curd into each bowl. Fill up with hot soup, sprinkle with ginger, cover with a lid and serve at once. This soup is a great favourite and, if correctly presented, is attractive both to the eye and the palate.

Note

Shrimps may be substituted for prawns.

ZONI
JAPANESE NEW YEAR SOUP

This rice cake soup is a New Year festival dish and it is traditionally said that only wakamizu, 'young water' drawn at break of dawn on New Year's day, is fit for this speciality. However, practice has proved that ordinary water is perfectly adequate, given the other ingredients and the necessary skill in preparation.
It is essential to observe the rules of presentation in order to conform to tradition. Taro, spinach and carrots, must be cut as described. If these vegetables

are chopped up or cut roughly they will make some sort of a soup, but it will not deserve the dignity of being called Zoni.

Preparation time 35 minutes
Cooking time 20 minutes
To serve 4

You will need

6 oz. uncooked breast of chicken
1 teaspoon cornflour
large piece kamaboko fish cake
1 carrot
2 taro roots, peeled
1¾ pints (U.S. 4¼ cups) dashi (see page 24)
soya sauce
salt
2 oz. spinach
lemon peel
8 o-mochi (glutinous rice cakes)

Cut the chicken into 8 uniform pieces and flatten slightly. Dip in cornflour and drop into a pan of boiling water, reduce heat and leave to simmer, so gently that the movement of the water is barely perceptible, until done – about 10 minutes.
Cut the kamaboko into 8 cubes. Cut the carrot into 8 slices, then into the shape of cherry blossom (see Cherry Blossom Carrots, page 41). Cut taro lengthways into 12 slices.
Boil carrot and taro in just enough dashi to cover, until soft – about 5 minutes. Season with soya sauce and salt to taste.
Cook spinach for 2 minutes in boiling salted water, drain, cut into 1-inch lengths. Cut lemon peel into 4 thin 'leaves', making sure all pith is shaved off.
Heat o-mochi rice cakes under the grill without allowing them to colour.
Bring remaining dashi to the boil, season with 1 teaspoon soya sauce and a pinch of salt.
Into each bowl put 2 o-mochi cakes, 2 slices of chicken, 2 cubes of kamaboko fish cake. Divide the vegetables equally, fill up the bowls with piping hot dashi, float a lemon peel 'leaf' on top, cover with lid, and serve.

NIMONO
BOILED DISHES

CUCUMBER STUFFED WITH CHICKEN

Preparation time 25 minutes
Cooking time about 30 minutes
To serve 4–6

You will need

12 small cucumbers
1 tablespoon oil
1 tablespoon white sesame seeds
8 oz. uncooked chicken, minced
1 tablespoon minced spring onion
1 red sweet pepper, deseeded and minced
2 tablespoons soya sauce
1 teaspoon sugar
1½ teaspoons salt
1 teaspoon monosodium glutamate
1 pint (U.S. 2½ cups) dashi (see page 24)
1 heaped teaspoon cornflour
1 tablespoon cold water

Cut tips off the cucumbers and make six incisions all round them, deep enough to hold stuffing, but not cutting right through the vegetable. Heat oil in a pan and fry the cucumbers all round without allowing them to brown.
Parch sesame seeds: i.e. heat them in a frying pan, without any fat, until they begin to 'jump'. Mix sesame seeds, chicken, onion, red pepper, soya sauce and sugar. Season with ½ teaspoon salt and ½ teaspoon monosodium glutamate, if liked. Stir well.
Stuff cucumbers by inserting chicken mixture into the slits. Press in carefully to prevent stuffing from falling out during cooking. When fully stuffed, the cucumbers should have a barrel-like shape with six bulging pockets.
Bring the dashi to the boil and add remaining salt and monosodium glutamate, if liked. Carefully put in the cucumbers and simmer until the chicken is cooked, about 20 minutes.
Lift out the cucumbers with a perforated spoon and keep hot on a dish. Blend the cornflour with the cold water, and stir into the stock, cooking until it thickens. Pour over the stuffed cucumbers and serve.

Note

Minced raw prawns may be substituted for the chicken, and courgettes for the cucumbers, if desired.

BOILED LOBSTER

Preparation time 20 minutes
Cooking time 10 minutes
To serve 4

You will need

2 lb. fresh lobster
4 tablespoons mirin *or* sweet white wine
4 tablespoons sake
3 tablespoons soya sauce
2½ teaspoons sugar

Cut off the lobster head and reserve. Cut off and discard tail tip. Wash lobster. Chop the main body into as many pieces as there are divisions in the shell. Split the head in half lengthways, removing sac, then cut each half across into three pieces. Cut off legs at first joint.
Pour wine, sake and soya sauce into a pan large enough to hold the lobster. Add sugar, blend well, and put in pieces of lobster head, pressing them in shell side down. Bring to the boil, add lobster body, shell side down. Finally, put in legs. Cover with a plate or smaller pan lid in such a way as to allow it to rest on the lobster pieces inside the pan. Cook briskly for 5 minutes, turning the pieces from time to time to ensure that all of them get coated with the sauce. Transfer to a serving dish, pour sauce over the lobster, and serve piping hot.

MUSHIMONO
STEAMED DISHES

There are two basic methods of steaming food in traditional Japanese cookery. The food is steamed in decorative individual bowls and served as it comes out of the steam kettle or bain-marie. Or it is steamed in a large pan, then put into individual small serving dishes.

CHAWAN-MUSHI
CUSTARD AND MUSHROOM SOUP

(Illustrated in colour on page 29)

This is, perhaps, the most famous of Japanese custard soups. Owing to the method of preparation this soup is frequently included under steamed dishes on menus.

Preparation time 35 minutes plus 25 minutes standing time
Cooking time 25–30 minutes
To serve 4

You will need

4 oz. uncooked chicken, sliced
soya sauce
2 oz. dried mushrooms
12 prepared gingko nuts or chestnuts
1¾ pints (U.S. 4¼ cups) dashi (see page 24)
salt
monosodium glutamate (optional)
4 eggs
½ kamaboko fish cake
12 trefoils (see page 24)
2 tiger lily bulbs
1 tablespoon vinegar
8 shrimps, peeled
2 thin slices lemon
2 fresh mushrooms (optional)
few peas (optional)

Sprinkle chicken with 1 tablespoon soya sauce and leave to stand for 15 minutes. Soak mushrooms in cold water for 10 minutes to soften; cut off and discard stalks. Shell and boil gingko nuts to remove outer layer of flesh. Heat dashi, season with salt, soya sauce and monosodium glutamate, if liked. Leave to cool.
Beat eggs, whisk into cold dashi, and strain. Cut kamaboko into neat slices diagonally. Tie trefoils into 4 bunches, as described in the recipe for Trefoil and Triangular Egg Soup (see page 24), dip into hot water for a second, drain and trim ends to a uniform length.
Peel the tiger lily bulbs. Place in a pan with 1 pint (U.S. 2½ cups) water and the vinegar, bring to the boil, strain and slice.
Divide ingredients, including the peeled shrimps, among 4 bowls. Decorate with trefoil bouquets and add half a slice of lemon to each. Fill with egg and dashi mixture, cover the bowls, and put in a steamer (or bain-marie) to steam until set (15–20 minutes). Serve in the same covered bowls garnished with half a mushroom and few cooked peas, if liked.

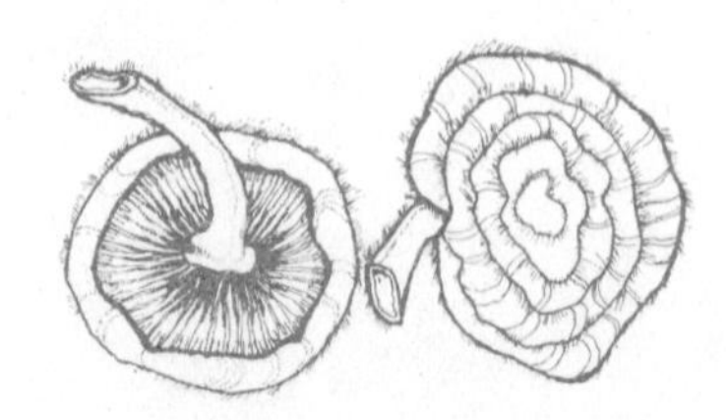

Custard and mushroom soup

Fresh scallops on ice (see recipes pages 38 and 71)

STEAMED EGG CUSTARD WITH BEAN CURD

Preparation time 10 minutes plus 10 minutes standing time
Cooking time 25 minutes
To serve 4

You will need

1½ pints (U.S. 3¾ cups) dashi (see page 24)
½ teaspoon soya sauce
½ teaspoon salt
2 eggs, beaten
4 pieces bean curd (tofu)

Flavour 4 tablespoons dashi with soya sauce and salt. Heat, stir and allow to cool; whisk into beaten eggs. Mash bean curd and whisk into egg mixture. Pour into a bowl and steam in a steam kettle or a bain-marie for 20 minutes. Slice into equal portions and serve either hot or cold in dashi.
In Japan this egg custard is often served with ice cubes and makes a very refreshing summer dish.

URAUCHI SHIITAKE
STUFFED MUSHROOMS

Preparation time 20 minutes plus 15 minutes standing time
Cooking time 27–28 minutes
To serve 6

You will need

36 dried mushrooms
2 teaspoons soya sauce
1 tablespoon sugar
½ pint (U.S. 1¼ cups) dashi (see page 24)
8 oz. peeled shrimps
1 egg white
1 teaspoon cornflour
salt
pinch monosodium glutamate (optional)

Soak mushrooms in cold water for 15 minutes to soften. Remove and discard stems.
Mix soya sauce, sugar and dashi; bring to the boil. Add mushrooms, simmer to permeate with the flavours of the mixture, remove from heat and drain. Mince the shrimps. Add egg white, cornflour, salt and monosodium glutamate to taste. Blend to a smooth paste. Stuff mushrooms with the shrimp filling, steam until shrimps are cooked.

MATSUTAKE DOBIN
STEAMED TREE MUSHROOMS

This is a great delicacy and there is a delightful and traditional way of presenting it. Each guest is provided with a dobin— a small teapot used for cooking tree mushrooms which are found in Japan in great abundance and are available in cans. In addition to a dobin each guest also requires a small wine cup, bowl-shaped and without handles, in which the cooking liquor is served.

Preparation time 15 minutes
Cooking time 24–26 minutes
To serve 4

You will need

4 large matsutake *or* tree mushrooms
1½ tablespoons sake
salt
4 oz. breast of chicken
4 oz. plaice fillet
bunch watercress
16 gingko nuts
½ pint (U.S. 1¼ cups) dashi (see page 24)
1 tablespoon soya sauce
1 tablespoon lemon juice
dash vinegar

Cut mushrooms into small dice, sprinkle with sake and season with small pinch salt. Cut chicken and plaice into small thin slices, put together on a dish and strain over them the liquid from the mushrooms. Shred watercress. Parch gingko nuts (i.e. heat in ungreased pan until they begin to 'jump'), remove hard outer shell, boil for a few minutes in slightly salted water and drain.
Divide mushrooms, chicken, plaice, nuts, watercress and dashi mixed with soya sauce, seasoned with ½ teaspoon salt, among 4 dobins. Steam for 20 minutes.
When serving, pour the liquid from each dobin into a wine cup provided for this purpose. Serve a small side dish of the lemon juice with the dash of vinegar added to it, for dipping morsels of food.
Note
Chestnuts may be used if gingko nuts are not available.

STEAMED SALTED HALIBUT

Preparation time 5 minutes
Cooking time 30 minutes
To serve 6

You will need

1 lb. halibut
1½ teaspoons salt
3 tablespoons soya sauce
1 tablespoon vinegar
1 tablespoon lemon juice
6 oz. grated radish
1–2 leeks, finely shredded

Wash halibut carefully, dry on a cloth and rub over with the salt. Put in an earthenware dish, steam for 30 minutes and serve very hot with small side dishes of soya sauce, vinegar, lemon juice, grated radish and shredded leeks. All these accompaniments are served separately and are for dipping mouthfuls of halibut in before eating.
Cod or hake may be substituted for halibut.

UNADAMA MUSHI
STEAMED EGG AND EEL SQUARES

Preparation time 10 minutes
Cooking time 50–55 minutes
To serve 6

You will need

EGG MIXTURE
8 eggs
¾ pint (U.S. 2 cups) dashi (see page 24)
6 grilled eels (see recipe for Unagi No Kabayaki, page 35)
1½ teaspoons soya sauce
pinch salt
pinch monosodium glutamate (optional)
pinch sugar

Mix all ingredients together, pour into a square mould or a biscuit tin and steam for 45 minutes. When cooked, turn out and cut into 2-inch squares.

SAUCE MIXTURE
¾ pint (U.S. 2 cups) dashi (see page 24)
½ teaspoon salt
1 teaspoon sugar
pinch monosodium glutamate (optional)
1 teaspoon cornflour
1 teaspoon cold water

Heat the dashi, add salt, sugar and monosodium glutamate. Blend the cornflour with the water, stir into sauce, cook until it thickens. Pour over the egg and eel squares and serve at once.
Note
Unagi No Kabayaki is available in cans, in which case the eels will require no cooking, just cutting to a convenient length of about ¼ inch.

TEMPURA
DEEP-FRIED DISHES

TEMPURA BATTER
FRYING BATTER

Preparation time 2–3 minutes
To serve 4

You will need

4 oz. unsifted flour
1 egg
½ pint (U.S. 1¼ cups) cold water

Mix flour, egg and water together, whisking lightly, without trying to make the mixture too smooth. A few lumps won't matter, as tempura batter is intended for immediate use. Never let it stand, and do not allow it to get warm.

Deep-fried prawns and vegetables

PRAWN AND VEGETABLE TEMPURA
DEEP-FRIED PRAWNS AND VEGETABLES

(Illustrated in black and white on page 32)

Preparation time 2–3 minutes
Cooking time 5–10 minutes
To serve 4

You will need

¾ pint (U.S. 1¾ cups) sesame oil
16 prawns, peeled
tempura batter (see page 32)
½ small onion, sliced
2 young carrots, sliced
tempura sauce (see below)
2 tablespoons grated ginger

This recipe is equally suitable for shrimps or crayfish.
Start heating oil slowly. Dip prawns in batter and fry first the prawns, then the vegetables. Serve with side dishes of tempura sauce and grated ginger. If serving in bowls with covers, place the prawns in such a way as to make the tail tips stick out.

TEMPURA SAUCE
SAUCE FOR FRIED FOOD

Cooking time 5 minutes
To serve 4

You will need

½ pint (U.S. 1¼ cups) dashi (see page 24)
4 tablespoons soya sauce
4 tablespoons sake *or* dry sherry
pinch monosodium glutamate (optional)

Bring dashi, soya sauce and sake to the boil, season with monosodium glutamate if liked, and serve in a side dish with Tempura dishes.

FISH TEMPURA
DEEP-FRIED PLAICE

Preparation time 20 minutes
Cooking time 5–10 minutes
To serve 4

You will need

4 fillets of plaice
salt and pepper
2½ tablespoons cornflour
¾ pint (U.S. 1¾ cups) sesame oil
1½ tablespoons lemon juice
½ teaspoon grated ginger
2 tablespoons soya sauce
4 oz. cucumber, sliced

Sole, cod, haddock, whiting or mackerel could all be used as alternative fish.
Wash fillets, dry on a cloth, cut into strips 1 inch wide and season with salt and pepper to taste. Mix cornflour with enough cold water to make a batter, dip fish in this and fry in hot oil. Make a dressing with the lemon juice, ginger and soya sauce and pour over fish.
Cut cucumber slices into strips and serve as a side dish.

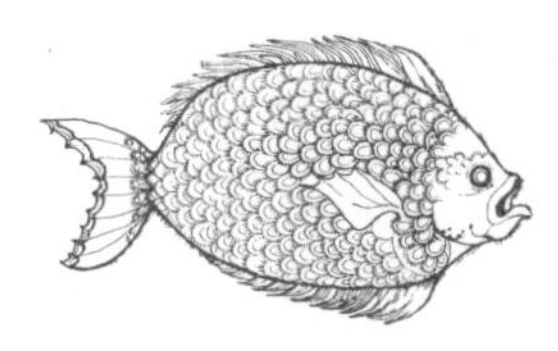

YAKITORI
GRILLS AND ROASTS

Grilling and open fire roasting are important and popular methods of Japanese cookery. All kinds of foods are cooked by this method: fish, chicken, meat, shellfish, vegetables. In particular, pork, lobsters and eels are frequently grilled.
Normally, the ingredients to be grilled or roasted are brushed with a mixture that is a combination of equal quantities of dashi or fish stock, sake and soya sauce before cooking. Certain foods are coated with diluted miso (bean paste) and left to stand for up to 48 hours before being grilled or roasted.
Pride of place among dishes of this category is the famous Yakitori Chicken – grilled chicken on skewers. Next to Sukiyaki, this is probably the most popular dish with westerners.

YAKITORI CHICKEN
GRILLED CHICKEN
(Illustrated in colour on page 11)

Preparation time	15 minutes
Cooking time	10–20 minutes
To serve	4

You will need

2 tablespoons soya sauce
2 tablespoons sake *or* sherry
1½ tablespoons sugar
6 oz. breast of chicken, diced *or* 4 chicken joints
4 oz. chicken giblets, diced (optional)
2 spring onions, sliced
1 or 2 sweet potatoes, peeled and sliced (optional)
4 oz. grated Japanese radish
1 teaspoon ground ginger
pepper

Mix the soya sauce, sake and sugar to make basting sauce and stir well.
Impale diced chicken, giblets, slices of onion and sweet potato on skewers. If using chicken joints, grill on their own and serve on a bed of salad.
Dip the skewered ingredients in the sauce and grill until brown on all sides, basting with the sauce. Mix radish with ginger, add a pinch of freshly ground pepper and dip each mouthful of chicken in this mixture before eating.

GRILLED MACKEREL

Preparation time	5 minutes plus 2 hours standing time
Cooking time	20 minutes
To serve	6

You will need

¼ pint (U.S. ⅔ cup) mirin *or* sweet white wine
5 tablespoons soya sauce
½ pint (U.S. 1¼ cups) dashi (see page 24)
6 mackerel fillets

Add half the wine and 3 tablespoons soya sauce to dashi and put the fillets to marinate in this mixture for 2 hours. Put the fillets on long skewers (for a wide piece of fish 2 skewers are recommended) and grill, basting with the marinade from time to time. Cook in 2 batches.
Bring the rest of the wine and soya sauce to the boil, simmer until mixture is reduced and thickened. Put the fillets on individual serving plates, pour thickened gravy over them, and serve.

PLAICE FILLETS WITH EGG YOLK AND MIRIN DRESSING

Preparation time	10 minutes plus 2 hours 15 minutes – 2 hours 20 minutes standing time
Cooking time	10 minutes
To serve	6

You will need

6 plaice fillets
salt
3 tablespoons sake *or* sherry
1 egg yolk
1 teaspoon mirin *or* sweet white wine
pinch monosodium glutamate (optional)

Sprinkle fillets with salt on both sides and leave for 2 hours. Rinse, wipe dry, sprinkle with sake. Leave to stand for 15–20 minutes for the sake to permeate the fish. Put on skewers and grill on both sides. Put on individual serving dishes and keep hot. Whisk egg yolk with wine and monosodium glutamate, if liked. Brush fish with this mixture and serve.

UNAGI NO KABAYAKI
GRILLED EELS

This dish forms the basis of a celebrated steamed dish, Eel and Egg Squares (see page 32).

Preparation time 15 minutes
Cooking time 9–10 minutes
To serve 4

You will need

8 small eels
salt
¼ pint (U.S. ⅔ cup) soya sauce
½ tablespoon mirin *or* sweet white wine
½ tablespoon sake *or* sherry
4 oz. sugar

Split the eels down the back, remove bones and cut flesh into ¼-inch lengths. Sprinkle with salt. Mix together the rest of the ingredients and boil the mixture for 2 minutes. Thread the eel pieces on skewers, dip in the sauce and cook on a hot grill for 7–8 minutes, brushing frequently with the sauce, turning to brown both sides, and being careful to fan the eels during grilling to prevent them catching fire. Serve very hot.

EELS ON SKEWERS

Preparation time 15 minutes
Cooking time 8–10 minutes
To serve 4

You will need

1 lb. eels
1½ pints (U.S. 3¾ cups) dashi (see page 24)
2 tablespoons sake *or* sherry
3 tablespoons soya sauce

Clean the eels, remove heads and bones. Add heads and bones to dashi and leave to simmer. Cut eels into portions, thread on skewers, lay on the grill skin side down. Add sake and soya sauce to dashi. Grill the eels until crisp and nicely browned, turning several times and basting with strained sauce. As eel flesh has a high fat content, to prevent it catching fire the fish should be fanned all the time during cooking. In Japan, a palm leaf fan is a kitchen utensil.

GRILLED CARROTS

Preparation time 15 minutes
Cooking time 7–8 minutes
To serve 4

You will need

1 lb. carrots
8 shelled peanuts
4 tablespoons dashi (see page 24)
1½ tablespoons sugar
2 tablespoons sake *or* sherry
2 egg yolks

Peel carrots, wash and cut into bite-sized chunks, then thread on long bamboo skewers. In a mortar pound peanuts to a smooth paste and put into a bowl. Gradually add dashi, sugar and sake. Stir egg yolks and blend into the mixture. Dip skewered carrots into this mixture, grill and serve. Turnips, aubergines, marrows and potatoes can be cooked by the same method.

GRILLED MUSSELS

Preparation time 15 minutes
Cooking time 8 minutes
To serve 5

You will need

20 mussels
5 tablespoons soya sauce
3 tablespoons mirin *or* sweet white wine

Scrub mussels well and rinse in several waters. Discard all those that are open. Heat in a pan for a few minutes until all have opened. Remove from shells. You will need 10 small skewers (bamboo, if possible). Thread 2 on each skewer. Boil soya sauce and wine together until the mixture thickens to a syrupy consistency. Dip mussels in this basting liquid, grill for 1 minute, then dip into the sauce again and return to the grill. Repeat twice more and serve. This recipe is also used in Japan for grilling oysters, clams, cockles and other similar shellfish.

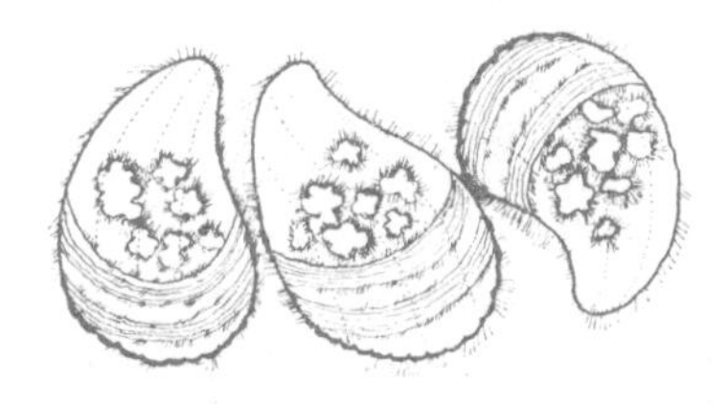

Grilled lamb chops

GRILLED LAMB CHOPS

(Illustrated in black and white above)

Preparation time	2–3 minutes plus overnight standing time
Cooking time	12 minutes
To serve	4

You will need

4 lamb chops
4 tablespoons soya sauce
4 tablespoons dashi (see page 24)
2 spring onions, chopped
1 tablespoon chopped fresh ginger *or* extra spring onion
½ cucumber, sliced

Put the chops in a small sauté pan. Mix the soya sauce, dashi and spring onions; bring to the boil, pour over the chops and leave to marinate in a cool place or refrigerator overnight.
Next day, drain the chops, and grill, turning once, on a low heat for 10 minutes, using the marinade as basting liquid. Brown both sides, garnish with the ginger or spring onion and serve with slices of cucumber.

PEPPERED PRAWNS

Preparation time	1 minute
Cooking time	9–10 minutes
To serve	2

You will need

6 large prawns, shelled
6 tablespoons mirin *or* sweet white wine
6 tablespoons soya sauce
freshly ground black pepper

Thread the prawns on two skewers. Boil wine and soya sauce until the mixture becomes syrupy. Grill the prawns, basting them with the sauce. Season to taste with pepper and serve.

Cucumbers

AEMONO AND SUNOMONO
SALADS AND DRESSINGS

The dressings are usually served in individual little dishes. Each guest uses chopsticks for dipping his food into his own dish of condiments.

COOKED SPINACH SALAD

Preparation time 5 minutes plus 10 minutes standing time
Cooking time 3 minutes
To serve 4

You will need

12 oz. fresh spinach
salt
sesame and soya dressing (see page 39)

Cut spinach into bite-sized pieces, wash carefully and boil in salted water for 3 minutes. Drain, cool and serve with the dressing.

MIMOSA SALAD

Preparation time 10 minutes plus 20 minutes standing time
Cooking time nil
To serve 4

You will need

8 oz. fresh white radish
4 oz. cucumber
salt
4 oz. peeled shrimps
egg dressing (see page 39)

Peel radish and cut into match-like strips. Cut cucumber similarly, without peeling. Sprinkle with salt, leave for 20 minutes, then gently squeeze out surplus liquid. Add shrimps. Mix well, pour egg dressing over the salad and serve.
The granulated appearance of the eggs gives the surface the 'mimosa' look and texture.

MUSSELS AND PICKLED ONION SALAD

Preparation time 5 minutes
Cooking time 2–3 minutes
To serve 4

You will need

12 oz. sliced pickled onions
water *or* dashi (see page 24)
12 oz. shelled fresh mussels, sliced
hot miso dressing (see page 38)

Boil onions in a little water or dashi for a few minutes, drain thoroughly, add mussels, mix lightly and serve with hot miso dressing in small individual bowls.
Note
This recipe is particularly recommended for all shellfish, such as scallops, cockles or oysters. It is also excellent for canned tunny, pilchards and sardines, transforming in a matter of minutes a mere can from your store cupboard into a satisfying, tasty meal.

RADISH, CARROT AND MUSHROOM SALAD

Preparation time 10 minutes plus 20 minutes standing time
Cooking time nil
To serve 4

You will need

8 oz. shredded radish
4 oz. shredded carrot
salt
8 dried mushrooms
egg dressing (see page 39)

Sprinkle radish and carrot with salt and leave to stand for 20 minutes to soften.
Soak mushrooms in warm water for 15 minutes, remove and discard stems. Cut caps into strips to match radish and carrot.
Squeeze out surplus liquid from radish and carrot, mix with mushrooms and serve with egg dressing.

SAKANA NITSUKE
SCALLOP AND CUCUMBER SALAD

(Fresh scallops illustrated in colour on page 30)

Preparation time 15 minutes plus 15 minutes standing time
Cooking time 2–3 minutes (optional)
To serve 4

You will need

4 scallops, shelled
1½ tablespoons vinegar
4 oz. cucumber
salt
2 tablespoons lemon juice
½ teaspoon soya sauce
3 tablespoons sake *or* sherry
2 teaspoons sugar

Clean the scallops in cold water, slice as thinly as possible, put into small serving bowls, sprinkle contents of each bowl with a dash of vinegar.
Keep in a refrigerator.
Cut the unpeeled cucumber into thin strips about 1½ inches long. Sprinkle with a small pinch salt and the remaining vinegar. Allow to stand for 15 minutes then use for garnishing scallops. Mix lemon juice, soya sauce, sake and sugar, stir well to blend all ingredients, pour this dressing over the salad and serve.

Note
This recipe is also recommended for clams, mussels and other shellfish. For those who dislike raw shellfish, scallops, clams or mussels can be boiled for 2–3 minutes, then chilled and treated as described above.

SOUSED MACKEREL SALAD

This recipe gives the opportunity to present a familiar fish in a uniquely different form.
No Japanese hostess would dream of serving soused mackerel slivers in any other form but raw. But, the mackerel could be steamed before being pickled in vinegar. Otherwise proceed exactly as described for Scallop and Cucumber Salad, page 38.

MISO DRESSING

Mash miso (fermented bean paste) into a smooth paste, add sugar and vinegar to taste and pour over the salad. The quantities depend on amount of dressing required but there is no danger of 'overdoing' the miso. Up to 1 oz. per portion may be allowed.

HOT MISO DRESSING

Preparation time nil
Cooking time 5 minutes
To serve 4

You will need

4 tablespoons miso or fermented bean paste
2 tablespoons sugar
2 tablespoons dashi (see page 24)
2 tablespoons vinegar

Heat miso in a small pan, add sugar and dashi, stir, gradually whisk in vinegar, remove from heat and serve.

SESAME AND SOYA DRESSING

Preparation time 2–3 minutes
Cooking time 2–3 minutes
To serve 4

You will need

2 tablespoons sesame seeds
2 tablespoons soya sauce

Either black or white sesame seeds may be used. Parch the sesame seeds (i.e. dry-fry them – without fat – in a pan until they begin to 'jump'), pound in a mortar, add soya sauce; pound together to amalgamate the dressing and serve.

SESAME DRESSING

Preparation time 5 minutes
Cooking time 2–3 minutes
To serve 4

You will need

3 tablespoons white sesame seeds
2 tablespoons vinegar
1 teaspoon salt
2 tablespoons sugar
1 tablespoon soya sauce
1 teaspoon lemon juice

Parch sesame seeds by dry-frying in an ungreased frying pan. Pound in a mortar, add rest of ingredients, pound for 2–3 minutes, mix well and serve in small dishes, one for each guest.

SESAME AND SUGAR DRESSING

Preparation time 5 minutes
Cooking time nil
To serve 4

You will need

3 tablespoons white sesame seeds, parched (see above)
1 tablespoon sugar

Pound sesame seeds, add sugar and pound together to mix. This dry dressing is principally used for salads and dishes with enough liquid in them.

EGG DRESSING

Preparation time 5 minutes plus 10 minutes standing time
Cooking time 3–4 minutes
To serve 4

You will need

2 eggs
1 teaspoon salt
1 tablespoon sugar
2 tablespoons vinegar

Beat eggs with salt and sugar, scramble in a saucepan over moderate heat. Immediately rub through a sieve, allow to cool, blend in vinegar and serve. This dressing should have a granulated appearance.

TSUKEMONO
PICKLED VEGETABLES

TAKUANZUKE
PICKLED RADISH

The daikon, one of many varieties of radish commonly found in Japan, is very different from the little round pink or purple ones so familiar to non-Asiatics. To begin with, it is long and white. The biggest specimens are up to 5 feet in length and weigh 20–30 lb. Both the root and the green tops are equally edible. It has excellent medicinal properties and the Japanese claim that they have no need of digestive tablets to 'settle their stomachs' because the daikon does it for them. Obviously a vegetable of such importance and reputation was bound to qualify for special treatment.
The classical method of pickling the daikon was invented, it is said, by a Buddhist priest called Takuan, and legend has it that the pickle owes its name of takuanzuke to the fact that the stone used as weight to press the daikon down in the cask resembled the stone on Takuan's grave in Tokyo.
The true takuanzuke is radish pickled in salt and

Peppers and chillis add spice to many dishes

rice bran and is served and eaten with relish all the year round.
There is an alternative radish salad, called asazuke, for which the daikon is pickled in salt and malt and left to ferment. Takuanzuke however deservedly retains pride of place among Japanese salads and here is a quick recipe for this outstanding speciality:

Preparation time	10–15 minutes plus 4 hours 10 minutes – 5 hours 15 minutes standing time
Cooking time	nil
To serve	4

You will need

1 lb. daikon
1½ tablespoons salt
rice bran (optional)
soya sauce
vinegar
fresh ginger, minced
red sweet pepper, finely sliced
dressing of choice (see pages 38–39)

Soak the daikon in cold water for 10–15 minutes, rinse and dry well. Cut off the leaves, chop into bite-sized pieces and rub with salt. Put the leaves in the bottom of the pickling jar. Slice and shred the radish and put into the jar in layers, sprinkling each layer with salt mixed with rice bran in equal proportions. (Just salt, if rice bran is not available.) Cover with a lid which must fit well inside the jar, put a heavy weight on top and leave for 4–5 hours, after which the takuanzuke is ready for use. Take out 2–3 tablespoons at a time, press out excess liquid and loosen with a fork or chopsticks. Serve the radish and the leaves with small side dishes (one for each guest) of soya sauce, vinegar, minced fresh ginger, finely sliced red pepper and one of the salad dressings.
Turnips, cabbage and cucumber can be prepared in the same way.

RINGO-ZUKE

Pickled apple rings. The apples are peeled and cored, then sliced, seasoned with salt (allowing 2½ teaspoons salt per pound of apples) and left to pickle for 2–3 months.

HAKUSAI

Pickled Chinese cabbage. The cabbage is cut up, sprinkled with salt (allowing 2½ teaspoons salt per pound of cabbage) and left to stand for a week.

PICKLED MIXED VEGETABLES

Radishes, cucumbers, aubergines and fresh mushrooms. As with most Japanese pickles, slice the vegetables, sprinkle in layers with salt (allowing 2½ teaspoons salt per pound of vegetables) and leave to stand for 2–3 months.

MAKUNOUCHI BENTO
BENTO LUNCH BOXES
(Illustrated in colour on page 47)

All the dishes given in this chapter are intended for packing into special bento lunch boxes. These boxes are usually made of lacquer ware, about 1 inch in depth, rectangular (about 6 inches long), square or round. Some have built-in partitions, with 'nests' for various types of food. A selection of dishes is packed into a bento box, with the ingredients arranged in separate groups, in the most attractive manner possible.
Sometimes a bento box is filled first with rice, then fish, pork, chicken, vegetables or eggs are laid on top in a pleasing pattern. A Japanese hostess might, for instance, offer her guests 3 bento boxes. The first box may contain grilled eel or sole fillets on a bed of cooked rice; the second may be chicken and egg on rice, or an assortment of vegetables; the third may be a selection of rice balls, egg roll slices, sweet boiled beans, sweet-sour shrimps or spinach rolls. The recipes which follow are all suitable for such treatment and are calculated for 6 persons, but the choice and the number of bento boxes to be served is left to your discretion. There is nothing to stop you filling a bento box with your favourite selection of Japanese dishes.

CHERRY BLOSSOM CARROTS

Preparation time 10 minutes
Cooking time 15–16 minutes
To serve 6

You will need

6 oz. carrots
$\frac{1}{4}$ pint (U.S. $\frac{2}{3}$ cup) dashi (see page 24)
3 teaspoons sugar
$\frac{1}{2}$ teaspoon salt
$1\frac{1}{2}$ teaspoons soya sauce

Choose fairly thick carrots, scrape or peel, cut into round slices about $\frac{1}{8}$ inch thick, then stamp out into cherry blossom shapes with a special cutter. Parboil in water for 2–3 minutes and drain. Mix dashi with sugar, salt and soya sauce, bring to the boil, add carrots and simmer gently until done. Do not overcook. Arrange in bento box.

Note

Experienced Japanese cooks are famous for their great skill in cutting vegetables and do not normally need any tools other than a selection of knives. Special cutters, however, can be bought or very small pastry cutters make adequate substitutes. Whatever the method, these small refinements are well worth while. Plain sliced carrots would look quite wrong in a bento box.

BENTO OMELETTE

Preparation time 10 minutes
Cooking time 10 minutes
To serve 6

You will need

2½ tablespoons dashi (see page 24)
1 teaspoon soya sauce
½ teaspoon salt
¼ teaspoon monosodium glutamate (optional)
2½ teaspoons sugar
3 eggs
oil

Add all ingredients (except oil) to the eggs and beat together. Heat a square frying pan, grease very lightly with oil and, using a third of the egg mixture, fry a flat omelette. As soon as top begins to set, roll up omelette, away from yourself, towards edge of pan. Leaving this rolled-up omelette at side of pan, brush over the pan with a little more oil, then using half the remaining egg mixture fry second omelette. Roll it around the first omelette, then in the same pan freshly greased, fry the third omelette with the rest of the egg mixture. Roll around the first two, making a thick omelette 'sausage' consisting of three layers of fried egg pancake. If the sausage is not regular in shape, roll it in a sudare (bamboo lattice mat) to give it an attractive neat appearance. If no mat is available, greased greaseproof paper may be used.
Leave until omelette roll is quite cold, then cut into slices.
These are appetising, good to eat cold, easy to handle and provide an interesting colour contrast arranged in a bento lunch box between, say, prawns and snow peas, or next to fried pork or beef.

GRILLED SOLE FILLETS

Preparation time 10 minutes plus 2–3 hours standing time
Cooking time 8–10 minutes
To serve 6

You will need

12 oz. sole fillets
salt

Cut fillets into 6 portions, brush with salt and leave for 2–3 hours. Rinse off salt, drain and gently mop up surplus moisture. Impale on skewers. Grill on both sides. Carefully extract skewers without damaging the fish, put on a dish and leave until cool before arranging on rice in a bento lunch box.

BENTO PORK

Preparation time 15 minutes plus 1 hour standing time
Cooking time 4–5 minutes
To serve 6

You will need

12 oz. lean pork
1½ tablespoons sake *or* sherry
1½ tablespoons soya sauce
cornflour
oil for deep frying

Cut the pork into strips about 2–2½ inches long. Mix the sake with soya sauce, pour over the pork, stir to mix well, and leave to marinate for 1 hour. Remove pork, drain off surplus liquid but do not wipe; the surface of the meat has to be slightly tacky. Roll each piece separately in cornflour. Deep-fry and drain off excess fat thoroughly. Arrange in bento box. Beef may be substituted for pork.

SNOW PEAS

Preparation time 8 minutes
Cooking time 9 minutes
To serve 6

You will need

6 oz. snow peas, *or* very young pea pods
1 teaspoon salt
3 tablespoons dashi (see page 24)
3 teaspoons sugar
¼ teaspoon monosodium glutamate (optional)

Wash the pods, drain, sprinkle with salt, boil in water for 1 minute, drain, rinse with cold water under a running tap. Shake out surplus liquid in a colander. Mix dashi with sugar, bring to boil, add monosodium glutamate if liked, and pinch of salt if necessary, put in peas, cook for 2 minutes, remove with perforated spoon and strain. Leave to cool. Cook down pan juices to thicken and then spoon over the peas. Put in bento box.

QUAIL EGGS WITH CHICKEN AND CHERRIES

Preparation time 30 minutes
Cooking time 23 minutes
To serve 6

You will need

12 quail eggs
6 oz. uncooked chicken, minced
salt
black pepper
1 egg, beaten
oil
2 tablespoons chicken stock (see page 24)
2 teaspoons sugar
3 teaspoons soya sauce
1 tablespoon mirin *or* sweet white wine
1 teaspoon cornflour
12 cherries, stoned
12 long cocktail sticks

Cook eggs in boiling water for 8 minutes. Dip in cold water and shell. Season chicken with salt and pepper to taste, stir in beaten egg to bind it, mix, shape into little pellets to match the size of quail eggs, and fry in oil to brown lightly on all sides. Mix stock, sugar, soya sauce and wine, bring to the boil, stir, put in chicken pellets and turn to lowest possible heat. Blend cornflour with just enough cold water to make a smooth paste, mix into the sauce, simmer to thicken, stirring gently. Remove from heat. Thread one egg, one chicken pellet and a stoned cherry on each cocktail stick and arrange in a bento lunch box.

NABE RYORI AND JUZUME
FIRESIDE AND FESTIVAL DISHES

CHICKEN SUKIYAKI
SAUCEPAN CHICKEN

This is a splendid Japanese institution. It is of Chinese origin and consists of dishes cooked before the eyes of the waiting guests, often called 'fireside', or 'friendship', meals.
Sukiyaki is an ideal dish for a party because all the preparation can be done in advance, the actual cooking does not have to start until the guests are safely assembled around the table.

Preparation time 25 minutes
Cooking time 20 minutes
To serve 4

You will need

2 medium onions
8 oz. spinach
1 crisp lettuce
1 lb. bean curd
16 fresh mushrooms
1 lb. uncooked chicken, thinly sliced
½ pint (U.S. 1¼ cups) dashi (see page 24)
¼ pint (U.S. ⅔ cup) soya sauce
6 oz. sugar
2 tablespoons sake *or* dry sherry
1 tablespoon chicken fat
boiled rice (see page 18)
4 eggs

Arrange vegetables and chicken on a large dish in separate groups, and place near the stove. Bear in mind that a pleasing presentation of these raw materials is a part of your table setting.
Heat together dashi, soya sauce, sugar and sake. Cut onions into bite-sized pieces. Tidy chicken, discard any discoloured spinach leaves, tear lettuce leaves into pieces. Cut bean curd into squares. Remove mushroom stalks. Grease pan with chicken fat, lay half the chicken in it in one layer, brown and turn. Move the chicken to one side, moisten with dashi mixture. Put in half the spinach, onions, lettuce, bean curd and mushrooms, but keep all the ingredients in separate groups. Turn carefully, so as not to transform contents of the pan into an indeterminate mixed fry.
Regulate the amount of each ingredient to be put in the pan at one time, making sure there is room for them all and that you have the correct amount for 4 servings.
Do not overcook the vegetables. As soon as they are done, taste for seasoning, adding more dashi mixture if necessary.
The characteristic flavour of Sukiyaki is a pleasant combination of sweet and sharp.
Serve with steaming rice as soon as the chicken is cooked. Serve 1 raw egg for each person in individual bowls. Each guest also has a small bowl of rice. They help themselves to whatever they like and dip the scalding hot ingredients into slightly beaten egg, which serves both as a dressing and to cool the food to just the right temperature to be enjoyed.
Prepare to cook the second helping while the first one is being eaten.

SOBA
COLD NOODLES
(Illustrated in black and white above)

Preparation time 3 minutes plus 1 hour standing time
Cooking time 10–15 minutes
To serve 6

You will need

12 oz. buckwheat noodles
3 pints (U.S. $7\frac{1}{2}$ cups) water
salt
18 trefoil or long watercress stems
$1\frac{1}{2}$ pints (U.S. $3\frac{3}{4}$ cups) dashi (see page 24)
$4\frac{1}{2}$ tablespoons soya sauce
2 tablespoons sugar
pinch monosodium glutamate (optional)
grated horseradish (see page 13)
ice cube (optional)

This is a traditional and attractive way of presenting cold noodles. Cook noodles in slightly salted water according to directions on packet. Drain, rinse with cold water, drain again and leave until quite cold – better still, chill in a refrigerator.
Tie trefoil in bundles of 3 and trim stems (see Trefoil and Triangular Egg Soup, page 24). Dip into boiling water for a moment, rinse with cold water and drain.
Mix dashi with soya sauce and sugar, add monosodium glutamate, bring to the boil, stir, remove from heat and chill. Garnish chilled noodles with trefoil or serve trefoil separately with grated horseradish. Add a cube of ice, if liked.
Pour chilled soup over noodles or serve separately.

BEEF KOBE
BEEF WITH MUSHROOMS AND AUBERGINES

Preparation time 20 minutes
Cooking time 7 minutes
To serve 6

You will need

1 lb. best rump steak
12 oz. mushrooms
8 spring onions
8 oz. aubergines
4 oz. celery
8 oz. bamboo shoots
$\frac{1}{2}$ pint (U.S. $1\frac{1}{4}$ cups) white radish juice (made of $1\frac{1}{2}$ lb. daikon radish)
$\frac{1}{2}$ pint (U.S. $1\frac{1}{4}$ cups) soya sauce
black pepper
monosodium glutamate (optional)
$\frac{1}{4}$ pint (U.S. $\frac{2}{3}$ cup) sake *or* sherry
3 tablespoons mirin *or* sweet white wine
$1\frac{1}{2}$ oz. sugar
2 oz. shredded suet

Slice beef, mushrooms, onions, aubergines, celery and bamboo shoots, as in recipe for Sukiyaki, arrange on plates, and put on the table in readiness for cooking. Grate the radish, squeeze out juice and strain, season with 1 tablespoon soya sauce, black pepper and monosodium glutamate to taste, and use this for dipping cooked food into before eating. Put a big frying pan to heat on a stove in the middle of the table. Mix rest of the soya sauce with sake and wine; add sugar and stir. Grease pan with suet. The guests dip any ingredient they choose into the soya sauce mixture and cook it in the frying pan.

Aubergines

PORK WITH PERSIMMON SAUCE

Preparation time 30 minutes plus 20 minutes standing time
Cooking time 20 minutes
To serve 4

You will need

8 oz. lean pork
salt
2 dried mushrooms
8 oz. bean sprouts
2 young carrots
4 tablespoons vinegar
12 oz. persimmons
2 teaspoons sugar
¼ teaspoon monosodium glutamate (optional)

Cut pork into bite-sized slices, sprinkle with pinch of salt, leave to stand for 5 minutes, boil in enough water to cover until tender, and drain. Soak mushrooms in water for 15 minutes, remove and discard stems, and cut into strips about the thickness of bean sprouts.

Boil bean sprouts in lightly salted water, and drain. Cut carrots into similar strips, sprinkle with salt and leave to soften, then drain off all liquid. Mix bean sprouts, mushrooms and carrots, add 1 tablespoon vinegar, stir, and drain off excess liquid. Add pork, and mix. Peel persimmons, remove seeds if any, mash pulp thoroughly, or put through a blender. Add remaining vinegar, sugar, monosodium glutamate, and salt to taste. Blend well, pour over pork and vegetables, mix, and serve.

TAGO MIKAN
TANGERINE BASKETS

This is a traditional Girls' Festival dish and a delicious way of serving tangerines.

Preparation time 20 minutes
Cooking time 5 minutes
To serve 4

You will need

4 tangerines
4 leaves gelatine
½ pint (U.S. 1¼ cups) water
4 oz. sugar

Cut each tangerine to make it look like a small basket with a handle on top. To do this, hold the tangerine stalk end up, make two parallel cuts ½ inch apart (less, if you want a more slender handle, though they tend to be rather fragile), on both sides of the top centre down to a third of the fruit from the top. Then, cut horizontally on each side of the handle and remove the two pieces cut out. Carefully extract the pulp and squeeze out its juice into a small bowl. You should now have a small-handled basket. Repeat the procedure for the rest of the tangerines. Melt gelatine in water, add sugar and tangerine juice, leave until jelly begins to set, spoon into tangerine baskets and chill.

Bento lunch box (see recipes pages 41–43)

Prawn cocktail, Bali style

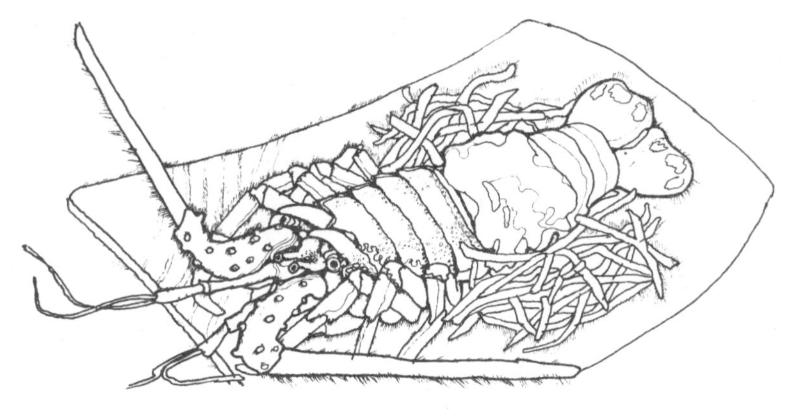

INDONESIA

The tropical islands which make up Indonesia abound in interesting foodstuffs and Indonesian cooking has a distinct and attractive personality. As in most Asian countries, rice is the staple item of food.
The Indonesian cook uses spices in much the same way as other cooks do in South East Asia. One feature which makes Indonesian cooking different is the popular use of peanut butter sauce, which is added to a great variety of dishes just before serving. The best known Indonesian speciality, still known by its Dutch name, Rijsttafel – meaning rice table – can be a banquet. Basically, it is a rice dish and it is the accompaniments – 20 to 30 dishes including sambals, pickles and chutneys – which make it so special.
In common with many other Asian countries desserts and sweets are few and fresh fruit is served in preference.

SELADA UDANG BALI
PRAWN COCKTAIL, BALI STYLE

(Illustrated in colour opposite)

Preparation time 10 minutes
Cooking time nil
To serve 4

You will need

½ lettuce, shredded
4 oz. peeled, cooked prawns
½ pint tomato mayonnaise (see right)
8 cooked, whole prawns
12 oysters, opened
lemon slices
parsley sprigs

Divide lettuce among 4 dishes. Mix the peeled prawns with half the tomato mayonnaise and divide this among the dishes. Garnish with the whole prawns. Put dishes on plates and surround each dish with oysters and lemon slices. Garnish with parsley. Serve rest of sauce separately.

LEMON AND OIL DRESSING

Preparation time 6 minutes

You will need

4 tablespoons olive oil
pinch salt and pepper
pinch paprika
2 tablespoons lemon juice

Mix oil and seasonings, drip in lemon juice gradually, stirring all the time to form an emulsion.

TOMATO MAYONNAISE

½ pint (U.S. 1¼ cups) mayonnaise
4 tablespoons tomato purée
1 tablespoon lemon juice
1 teaspoon grated lemon rind
salt and pepper to taste

Mix all ingredients together and use as required.

SAJUR
VEGETABLE SOUP

This is an Indonesian soup which can be part of the Rijsttafel menu (see page 56). It can be served in individual bowls or spooned over boiled rice.

Preparation time 20 minutes
Cooking time 25–30 minutes
To serve 8

You will need

2 onions, chopped
2 cloves garlic, crushed
1 teaspoon cumin
1 teaspoon coriander
1 teaspoon fresh sliced ginger
½ teaspoon chilli powder
1 bay leaf
1 dried lemon leaf
2 teaspoons salt
2 tablespoons peanut oil
3 pints (U.S. 7½ cups) coconut milk (see page 53)
1 carrot, shredded
4 oz. runner beans, sliced
6 oz. cabbage or Brussels sprouts, shredded
4 oz. shelled or frozen peas
small cauliflower, divided into flowerets
8 oz. lean beef, finely minced
1 teaspoon grated lemon rind
1 sweet pepper, deseeded and shredded
1 teaspoon paprika
pinch brown sugar
1 onion, finely sliced
8 oz. peeled prawns
3–4 tablespoons grated coconut

Blend in liquidiser or pound in a mortar chopped onions, garlic, cumin, coriander, ginger, chilli, bay leaf, lemon leaf and 1 teaspoon salt until all these ingredients are reduced to a smooth paste. Fry for 3 minutes in 1 tablespoon hot oil, stirring constantly. Add coconut milk, blend well and bring to the boil. Add carrot, beans, cabbage or sprouts, peas, cauliflower, beef, lemon rind and sweet pepper. Season with remaining salt and paprika, sprinkle with sugar. Cook over low heat for 15–20 minutes and make sure you have enough coconut milk in the pan to prevent drying out.
Fry the sliced onion in remaining oil until very crisp. Transfer Sajur into a serving bowl, garnish with prawns, fried onion and grated coconut and serve.

NASI GORENG
FRIED RICE

This is a delicious and satisfying dish, a meal in itself, excellent for using up leftovers of cooked meat, poultry, fish, prawns, ham and vegetables.

Preparation time 10 minutes plus 45 minutes standing time
Cooking time 30 minutes
To serve 4

You will need

8 oz. rice
generous ½ pint (U.S. 1½ cups) salted boiling water
2 oz. dried shrimps
¼ pint (U.S. ⅔ cup) peanut oil
2 onions, finely chopped
1 clove garlic, finely chopped
1 fresh chilli, shredded *or* ½ teaspoon chilli powder
8 oz. cooked meat, diced *or* chicken *or* fish *or* vegetables

SHREDDED OMELETTE
1 oz. butter
3 eggs, beaten
salt and pepper
cucumber, thinly sliced

Wash rice, add to boiling water and cook for 10 minutes. Drain thoroughly, spread on a large dish and leave to cool. Soak the dried shrimps (available from Chinese food shops) for 45 minutes in enough water to cover.
Heat oil in a large frying pan or a Chinese wok. Fry the onions until they turn transparent. Add garlic and chilli, fry for 3 minutes. Add meat and fry for 2 minutes, stirring all the time. Add rice. Drain shrimps and add to pan. Fry quickly, stirring frequently, until the rice turns a pale golden colour. Season to taste. Put on a heated serving dish and keep hot.
Heat butter in frying pan, stir in beaten eggs, seasoned with salt and pepper to taste. Cook gently on both sides. Take out of pan and shred finely. Arrange on top of the rice, garnish with cucumber and serve piping hot.

BAHMI GORENG
FRIED NOODLES

Preparation time 10 minutes
Cooking time 25–30 minutes
To serve 6

You will need

8 oz. Chinese egg noodles
$\frac{1}{4}$ pint (U.S. $\frac{2}{3}$ cup) peanut oil
12 oz. pork, finely shredded
2 cloves garlic, crushed
1 large onion, sliced
2 teaspoons finely grated green ginger *or* 3 teaspoons powdered ginger
2–3 sticks celery, chopped
1 lb. cabbage, shredded
4 oz. peas *or* beans
3 oz. bean sprouts
8 oz. cooked, peeled prawns
1 tablespoon soya sauce
8–10 spring onions, chopped
salt
black pepper, freshly ground
shredded omelette (see page 50)

Cook the noodles in plenty of boiling salted water for 5–6 minutes, drain; spread out on a board and leave to cool and dry. Heat 1–2 tablespoons oil and brown the pork lightly for 5 minutes. Remove from pan and keep warm. Add another tablespoon oil to pan and fry the garlic, onion and ginger for 3 minutes. Remove and keep warm.
Add 2 tablespoons oil and lightly fry celery, cabbage, peas or beans and bean sprouts for 2–3 minutes. Remove and keep warm.
In the same pan quickly toss the prawns for 1 minute. Add pork, and all the other fried ingredients. Sprinkle with soya sauce and spring onions, season to taste with salt and pepper, mix well and cook for 2 minutes.
Heat the remaining oil in another pan and fry the noodles until pale golden. Transfer to a heated serving dish. Pile the mixture of fried pork, vegetables and prawns on top. Garnish with shredded omelette and serve with boiled rice and Indonesian pickles (see Atjar page 60).

SELADA UDANG DAN PISANG
PRAWN AND BANANA SALAD, JAVA STYLE

Preparation time 20 minutes
Cooking time 20 minutes
To serve 6

You will need

6 oz. Patna rice
1 pint (U.S. $2\frac{1}{2}$ cups) chicken stock
2 tablespoons olive oil
1 tablespoon lime *or* lemon juice
4 sticks celery, chopped
salt and pepper
lettuce
1 lb. peeled, cooked prawns
4 tablespoons lemon and oil dressing (see page 49)
4 tablespoons coconut milt (optional) (see page 53)
4 bananas, halved lengthways
6 hard-boiled eggs, halved
$\frac{1}{2}$ lb. ripe tomatoes, peeled and sliced
$\frac{3}{4}$ pint (U.S. 2 cups) tomato mayonnaise (see page 49)

Boil the rice in the stock for 20 minutes or until cooked. Drain and, while still hot, add oil and lime or lemon juice; mix well and allow to cool completely. When cold, add celery, mix well, check seasoning.
Line a serving dish with crisp lettuce leaves, heap the rice in a dome in the middle. Toss the prawns in lemon and oil dressing mixed with coconut milk and sprinkle some of the dressing on bananas. Garnish the rice with prawns, bananas and hard-boiled eggs. Make a border of tomato slices, overlapping slightly around the outer edge of the dish. Put the tomato mayonnaise in a Chinese soup bowl, slightly flatten the dome of rice, implant bowl in the centre and serve.

KNEADED BUTTER

Beat together $2\frac{1}{2}$ teaspoons butter and $1\frac{1}{2}$ teaspoons flour. Continue beating until mixture has become a smooth paste. Use as required.

AJAM DISADJIKAM DALAM KELAPA
CHICKEN IN COCONUT, BALI STYLE
(Illustrated in black and white below)

Preparation time	20 minutes plus 3 hours standing time
Cooking time	1 hour 30 minutes–1 hour 45 minutes
Oven temperature	149°C., 300°F., Gas Mark 2
To serve	4

You will need

4 fresh coconuts
1 pint (U.S. 2½ cups) water
1½ oz. butter
1 onion, chopped
1 clove garlic, pounded
12 oz. raw chicken, sliced
2 green sweet peppers, sliced
4 oz. tomatoes, peeled and sliced
salt and pepper
1 teaspoon kneaded butter (see page 51)
flour
water
4 tablespoons white rum

Get your greengrocer to saw off the tops of the coconuts, but keep the 'lids'. Extract the coconut flesh and soak half in water for 3 hours, to soften and make it yield up its milk. Squeeze out two or three times to get as much thick milk as you can – you need about ½ pint (U.S. 1¼ cups). Shred the remaining coconut flesh.

Turn on the oven at the temperature given above. Heat the butter and lightly cook the onion and the garlic until soft. Add chicken, green peppers; cook, stirring constantly for 5 minutes, then add tomatoes, shredded coconut and salt and pepper to taste. Pour in coconut milk, cover and simmer for 20 minutes. Check seasoning, make a liaison by incorporating a little kneaded butter.

Make a thickish paste with some flour and water. Fill the coconut shells with the cooked chicken and its sauce, then carefully put the 'lids' on again, sealing them with the flour and water paste.

Put into a baking tin with a little water to come about quarter-way up the coconuts, and cook in the preheated oven for 1 hour–1 hour 15 minutes. Spoon a little water over the sealed coconuts from time to time to prevent them burning.

Remove from pan, dry off the bottoms on a cloth, put each coconut on a serving plate, take off 'lids', pour a tablespoon of rum over each coconut, set alight and serve.

Note

Lobster can be substituted for chicken – use 12 oz. sliced, shelled lobster meat. (Illustrated in colour on page 2.)

OPOR AJAM
COCONUT CHICKEN

Preparation time	10 minutes
Cooking time	30–35 minutes
To serve	4

You will need

1 onion, finely sliced
1 clove garlic, chopped
½ coconut, shelled and shredded
2 tablespoons oil
12 oz. cooked chicken, diced
¼ teaspoon chilli powder
1 teaspoon grated fresh ginger
1–2 teaspoons ground coriander
1 pint (U.S. 2½ cups) coconut milk (see page 53)
salt

Fry the onion, garlic and shredded coconut in oil. Remove from heat and transfer to a casserole. Add the chicken, chilli, ginger, coriander, coconut milk and salt to taste. Mix well. Bring to the boil, reduce heat, simmer gently, uncovered, for 15–20 minutes.

Chicken in coconut, Bali style

SAN TAN
COCONUT MILK AND COCONUT CREAM
(Using fresh coconut)

Preparation time 15 minutes plus 3 hours standing time

You will need

1–2 fresh coconuts (depending on how much liquid is required)
water

Pierce two of the 'eyes' at the sharp end of each coconut, using a red-hot skewer and extract and discard the water inside.
Crack the coconut with a hammer or saw it in half. Take out and grate the white flesh. Measure the grated coconut in a cup and put it in a bowl. Add twice as much water – i.e. 2 cups water to 1 cup coconut. Mix well and leave for 3 hours to soften.
Put the soaked coconut flesh in a muslin bag and squeeze out as much liquid as possible. This first pressing is thicker than succeeding pressings. To differentiate I have referred to it in recipes as *coconut cream.*
Return the coconut to the bowl, mix well and repeat the pressing. This and further pressings are *coconut milk.*
If preferred, put soaked coconut and liquid through a blender.

SAN TAN
COCONUT MILK
(Using dried or desiccated coconut)

Preparation time 5 minutes plus 15 minutes standing time

You will need

desiccated coconut
water *or* milk *or* ½ water and ½ milk

Allow 4 oz. coconut to ½ pint (U.S. 1¼ cups) water or milk.
Put coconut in a bowl and pour liquid over. Stir well and allow to stand for 15 minutes. Press in a muslin bag as described in the recipe using fresh coconut (see above). Repeat as required.

Note
If preferred, put soaked coconut and liquid through a blender.

PISANG GORENG
CRISPY BANANAS

Preparation time 5 minutes
Cooking time 2–3 minutes
To serve 4

You will need

peanut oil for deep frying
3–4 ripe bananas
lemon juice
2–3 tablespoons brown sugar

Heat the oil. Peel and cut bananas in half lengthways, dip in lemon juice, coat with brown sugar and fry until crisp and golden. Drain on absorbent paper and serve at once.

GULA MALACCA
SAGO PUDDING
(Illustrated in colour on page 57)

Preparation time 5 minutes
Cooking time 15–20 minutes
To serve 6

You will need

8 oz. sago
½ pint (U.S. 1¼ cups) coconut cream (see page 53)
salt
4 oz. brown sugar *or* palm sugar cut up

Bring 1 pint (U.S. 2½ cups) water to a fast boil. Add sago and cook, stirring, until the mixture thickens to a paste.
Remove from heat and put into a rinsed mould or into individual serving dishes. Leave to cool. Now proceed to make the sauces. First, gently heat the coconut cream. Season with a little salt and simmer until it thickens. Remove from heat, pour into a serving jug and leave to cool. For the second sauce, put the sugar in a pan with ¼ pint (U.S. ⅔ cup) boiling water. Simmer stirring, until syrup thickens slightly.
Remove from heat and allow to cool. Turn out the sago as you would a jelly out of the mould or serve in individual dessert dishes. Pour some of each sauce over the Gula Malacca and serve.
It is the two sauces which make this dish particularly delicious.

SATE
INDONESIAN SATAY
(Illustrated in colour on page 58)

This is an Indonesian speciality, but popular also in parts of South China and Malaya. Street vendors in Java sell them the way hot dogs are sold in America, but to me satay are much more tempting. They are a variation on all the kebabs. The meat is cut into bite-sized cubes, steeped in a special marinade almost always containing creamy Coconut Milk (see page 53), threaded on small bamboo or palm leaf skewers, grilled and served with Satay Sauce (see below).
Satay can be made of beef, veal, pork, any kind of poultry or chicken livers.
About 6 pieces of meat are threaded on one skewer and 2 skewers are usually allowed per portion. Skewers of piping hot Satay, with a bowl of Satay Sauce handed separately, make splendid cocktail food.

BUMBU SATE TIDAK DENGAN MINJAK
SATAY SAUCE (1) without oil

Preparation time 10 minutes
Cooking time 5 minutes
To serve 4

You will need

4 oz. roasted peanuts
1 clove garlic, crushed
1 onion, sliced
2 fresh chillis, deseeded, *or* ½ teaspoon chilli powder
½ teaspoon tamarind (in a piece, if available)
1 teaspoon sugar
2 tablespoons lime *or* lemon juice
2 tablespoons coconut cream (see page 53)
2 tablespoons water
1 tablespoon soya sauce

Put peanuts, garlic, onion, chillis, tamarind and sugar in a mortar and pound to a paste (or blend in a liquidiser). Blend in lime or lemon juice, then the coconut cream. Add water and soya sauce, stir well. Transfer to a saucepan, simmer gently until the sauce thickens.
Serve with all satay dishes.

BUMBU SATE DENGAN MINJAK
SATAY SAUCE (2) with oil

Preparation time 5 minutes
Cooking time 10 minutes
To serve 4

You will need

2 onions
1–2 tablespoons peanut oil
3 oz. roasted peanuts
½ teaspoon chilli powder
¼ pint (U.S. ⅔ cup) warm water
1 teaspoon brown sugar
salt
1 tablespoon soya sauce
juice of ½ lime *or* lemon

Slice 1 onion and fry in hot oil. Chop the second onion finely, put in a mortar with peanuts and chilli powder and pound to a paste (or blend in a liquidiser). Add the paste to the fried onion and fry together for 3 minutes, stirring well. Gradually add the warm water; stir in the sugar. Cook for a few minutes to concentrate the sauce so that it has the consistency of single cream. Season with salt to taste, add soya sauce and lime or lemon juice. Mix well and use for basting or serving with all satay dishes.

SATE LEMBU
VEAL SATAY

Preparation time 10 minutes plus 2 hours standing time
Cooking time 10 minutes
To serve 4

You will need

1 tablespoon ground almonds
1 small piece of root ginger, sliced
1 teaspoon coriander
1 teaspoon turmeric
½ pint (U.S. 1¼ cups) coconut milk (see page 53)
1 lb. veal
salt and pepper
1 teaspoon brown sugar

Pound the almonds, ginger, coriander, and turmeric to a paste, gradually blend with coconut milk. Cut the veal into bite-sized cubes, season to taste with salt and freshly ground pepper, put into spiced coconut milk, and leave to marinate for 2 hours. Remove pieces of veal, impale on skewers, sprinkle with sugar and grill, turning often and basting frequently with the coconut liquid. Serve with Satay Sauce (see page 54).

SATE LEMBU
BEEF SATAY

Follow recipe for Veal Satay, substituting fillet of beef for veal. Allow 4–5 pieces of beef to each skewer, grill, turning often and basting with the marinade. Dip in Satay Sauce (see page 54) just before serving. Serve the rest of the sauce separately.

SATE AJAM DENGAN BUMBU KATJANG
INDONESIAN CHICKEN SATAY WITH PEANUT BUTTER SAUCE

Preparation time	20 minutes plus 1 hour standing time
Cooking time	25 minutes
To serve	4–6

You will need

$3\frac{1}{2}$-lb. chicken, boned
$1\frac{1}{2}$ teaspoons salt
freshly ground black pepper
$\frac{1}{4}$ pint (U.S. $\frac{2}{3}$ cup) coconut cream (see page 53)
3–4 tablespoons peanut butter
1 teaspoon chilli powder
1 teaspoon grated lemon rind
$1\frac{1}{2}$ teaspoons brown sugar
generous $\frac{1}{2}$ pint (U.S. $1\frac{1}{2}$ cups) hot water
juice of $\frac{1}{2}$ lime *or* lemon

Cut the chicken into 1-inch pieces. Combine salt, pepper and coconut cream in a dish, put the chicken into it and leave to marinate (about an hour). Skewer and grill, basting with the marinade. Put peanut butter, chilli powder, lemon rind, sugar and water into a saucepan, bring to the boil, then reduce heat and simmer for 15 minutes. Remove from heat, stir in lime juice, spoon a little over each skewer and serve the rest in a sauceboat.

Indonesian satay

RIJSTTAFEL
RICE TABLE

This is a great Indonesian dish, a vast banquet in itself. Allow yourself and your guests plenty of time to enjoy it, for it is not to be approached as a hasty snack.
The basis is a dish of impeccably boiled rice, used as a canvas for a splendid piece of culinary embroidery. It is the delicious accompanying side dishes, satays and sambals which demand your attention. At a good Java or Bali restaurant there might be as many as 30–40 of these side dishes and each deserves to be sampled.
Most of the side dishes can be prepared in advance and having cooked your Rijsttafel you need do no more – nothing, except fruit for the stalwart, could possibly follow it.
Serve cold light beer or lager to drink with the Rijsttafel.
All the side dishes are served at the same time, but each on a separate dish. A morsel or spoonful of each is put on each plate, on a bed of steaming snowy rice. I have left out the number of servings each dish gives, as this depends so much on the number of side dishes being offered.

TELUR ASIN
PRESERVED DUCK EGGS

This is a Chinese delicacy and an essential part of Rijsttafel. In China duck eggs are preserved in a solution of salt, lime and soda or potash. They can be bought ready for use in Chinese food shops. In Java they are dipped in salt water solution, dried and buried in a flower pot for anything from 10–30 days.
Hard-boil, shell and cut in half before serving.

SOTO AJAM
CHICKEN WITH VERMICELLI

Preparation time 25 minutes
Cooking time 3 hours 3 minutes

You will need

4-lb. boiling chicken
salt
1 teaspoon turmeric
1-inch piece of green ginger, chopped
2–3 cloves garlic, chopped
1 onion, chopped
1–2 tablespoons peanut oil
2 oz. Chinese vermicelli
10–12 spring onions, chopped

Simmer the chicken in salted water to cover until tender – about 2 hours 30 minutes. Remove and bone the chicken. Return the bones to the stock once the meat has been removed. Boil the stock until it is reduced by half. Cut meat in slices.
Pound the turmeric, ginger, garlic and onion, with a pinch of salt in a mortar (or reduce to a paste in a blender). Fry the mixture in hot oil for 3 minutes.
Strain the stock, add meat, stir in spice paste, bring to the boil and simmer, uncovered, for 10 minutes.
Add Chinese vermicelli and boil fast for 5 minutes.
Check seasoning and add salt, if necessary. Sprinkle with spring onions, cook for 5 minutes and serve.

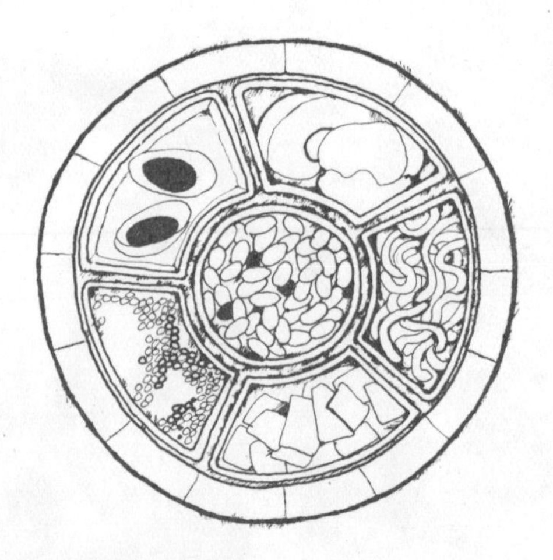

Sago pudding (see recipe page 53)

Indonesian satay (see recipes pages 54–55)

KARI AJAM
CHICKEN CURRY
(Illustrated in colour on front cover)

Preparation time 5 minutes
Cooking time 40 minutes

You will need

4 joints chicken
2 teaspoons salt
3 oz. butter
2 medium onions, sliced
1 teaspoon chilli powder
½ teaspoon turmeric
1 teaspoon curry powder
1 teaspoon ginger
2 cloves garlic, crushed
1 pint (U.S. 2½ cups) coconut milk (see page 53)
few slices green sweet pepper

Rub the chicken joints with the salt. Heat the butter in a frying pan and gently fry the onions until translucent. Remove onions from the pan and add the chilli powder, turmeric, curry powder, ginger and garlic. Cook gently for a few minutes. Add chicken and fry on all sides until golden. Add the onions and the coconut milk. Simmer, covered, for about 20 minutes or until tender. Remove lid and cook for a further 5 minutes. Garnish with pepper slices.
Serve with rice, Apple and Mint Sambal (see page 63) and Mixed Fruit Chutney (see page 63).

HATI GORENG
FRIED LIVER

Preparation time 5 minutes
Cooking time 7–8 minutes

You will need

2–3 tablespoons peanut oil
1 onion, finely chopped
1 clove garlic, finely chopped
1 lb. calves' liver, cut in thin strips
salt

Heat the oil and fry onion and garlic. As soon as these are cooked, move them to one side and quick-fry the liver on high heat for 2–3 minutes. Just before serving, sprinkle with salt.

IKAN BUMBU PEDAS
SPICED FISH FILLETS

Preparation time 5 minutes
Cooking time 9–10 minutes

You will need

1 lb. fish fillets (mullet for preference)
walnut-sized piece of tamarind
3–4 tablespoons peanut oil
2 onions, finely chopped
2 cloves garlic, finely chopped
½ teaspoon finely chopped fresh chilli (optional)
1 tablespoon soya sauce
2 tablespoons water
1 teaspoon soft brown sugar
juice of 1 lime *or* lemon

Rub the fish fillets with tamarind, then fry them in hot oil to brown both sides. Reduce heat, add onions and garlic and cook for 3–4 minutes. Add chilli and fry lightly. Mix soya sauce, water, sugar and lime or lemon juice and pour over the fish. Bring to the boil, simmer for 3–4 seconds only and serve.

WHITE SAUCE

Preparation time 1 minute
Cooking time 8 minutes

You will need

2 oz. butter
2 oz. flour
1 pint (U.S. 2½ cups) milk
salt and pepper

Melt the butter over low heat, stir in flour, and cook gently for 3 minutes, stirring all the time, and without allowing it to colour, if you want your white sauce to be white. Remove from heat, blend in half the milk, return to heat, and cook gently, stirring until the sauce thickens, then add the rest of the milk. Continue to cook, and beat the sauce until the desired consistency is reached. Season to taste, stir, and use at once.

ATJAR
VEGETABLE PICKLE

Preparation time 10 minutes
Cooking time 14–15 minutes

You will need

1 carrot, finely sliced
2 green sweet peppers, deseeded and finely sliced
1 cucumber, finely sliced
4 oz. runner beans, sliced
8 oz. shallots
salt
4–5 blanched cashew nuts or almonds
1 teaspoon turmeric
2 cloves garlic
1-inch slice of fresh green ginger
1 pint (U.S. $2\frac{1}{2}$ cups) vinegar
1–$1\frac{1}{2}$ tablespoons brown sugar

Drop the carrot, peppers, cucumber, beans and shallots into enough boiling salted water to cover, boil for 4–5 minutes and drain well.
Pound in a mortar the nuts, turmeric, garlic and ginger, or blend in a liquidiser, to reduce them to a smooth paste. Gradually add the vinegar and $\frac{1}{4}$ pint (U.S. $\frac{2}{3}$ cup) water. Season with salt to taste. Add sugar, mix well and bring to the boil. Add parboiled vegetables, cook for 10 minutes.
Allow to cool then chill. Serve cold.

Lamb vindaloo

KAMBING BUMBU VINDALOO
LAMB VINDALOO

(Illustrated in black and white below)

Preparation time 10 minutes plus 1–2 hours standing time
Cooking time 10–15 minutes

You will need

$1\frac{1}{2}$ lb. lean lamb
vindaloo paste (see below)
salt
$\frac{1}{4}$ pint (U.S. $\frac{2}{3}$ cup) vinegar
water
lemon slices
1 spring onion, finely chopped

Trim and cut the meat into bite-sized pieces. Blend with the vindaloo paste, season with salt to taste, add the vinegar, mix well and leave to macerate for 1–2 hours.
Fry without adding any fat, but moistening with a few tablespoons of water, as required. Stir frequently. As soon as the lamb is tender, serve, garnished with lemon slices and spring onion.

SAMBAL VINDALOO
VINDALOO PASTE

Preparation time 5 minutes

You will need

5–6 fresh red chillis, deseeded
$\frac{1}{2}$-inch slice fresh green ginger
$1\frac{1}{2}$ teaspoons ground coriander
1 teaspoon cumin
1–2 cloves garlic, crushed
$\frac{1}{4}$ teaspoon ground turmeric

Combine all ingredients and pound in a mortar or blend in a liquidiser to make a smooth paste. Use as required.

ABON
FRIED MEAT

This is a Rijsttafel must – but be sure to start preparations 24 hours before the dish is required.

Preparation time 20 minutes plus overnight standing time plus 3 hours
Cooking time 1–2 hours

You will need

1 lb. lean beef
1 clove garlic
1 onion
small piece tamarind
1 teaspoon coriander
1 teaspoon soft brown sugar
small pinch chopped green ginger
salt
2–3 tablespoons peanut oil

Bring the beef to the boil in barely enough water to cover. Simmer until tender, allow to cool; shred. Leave overnight.
Next morning grind and pound in a mortar the garlic, onion, tamarind and coriander. Add the sugar, ginger and salt. Mix well and rub the mixture into the meat. Leave for 3 hours, turning the meat from time to time.
Heat the oil and fry the meat until crisp.

RIJSTTAFEL DAGING LEMBU
BEEF, JAVA STYLE
(Illustrated in black and white above)

Preparation time 5 minutes
Cooking time 25–30 minutes

You will need

1 lb. frying steak
2 tablespoons peanut oil
2 medium onions
1 clove garlic, grated
salt
small pinch chilli powder
$\frac{1}{4}$ pint (U.S. $\frac{2}{3}$ cup) coconut milk (see page 53)
few slices red sweet pepper

Cut the meat into bite-sized pieces and brown lightly in the oil. Chop onions, and add to pan with garlic, salt and chilli powder. Mix well, and cook until onions turn pale golden. Add coconut milk, stir, simmer for 15–20 minutes, and serve, garnished with slices of sweet pepper.

Beef, Java style

KEMANGI
DEEP-FRIED MEAT BALLS

Kemangi are a classic Rijsttafel side dish.
They can be made of any good cooked – but not over-cooked – meat: beef, veal, pork, or chicken. They are delicious made of ham, prawns or mushrooms. More than one kind of Kemangi is sometimes served at a Rijsttafel meal.

Preparation time 25 minutes
Cooking time 12–16 minutes

You will need

8 oz. cooked meat or chicken (see above)
$\frac{1}{2}$ quantity white sauce (see page 59)
salt and pepper
juice of $\frac{1}{2}$ lime or lemon
$1\frac{1}{2}$ teaspoons chopped parsley
peanut oil for deep frying
flour
1–2 eggs, beaten
breadcrumbs

Mince the meat. Make the white sauce. When it thickens, check seasoning and stir in lime juice. Remove from heat, add meat and parsley, mix well and spread the Kemangi mixture on a shallow dish to cool.
Put oil to heat.
Taking teaspoons of the mixture, shape into little balls, roll in flour, dip in beaten egg, coat with breadcrumbs and deep-fry in oil until golden. Drain on absorbent paper and serve with Satay Sauce (see page 54) in a separate sauce boat.

AJAM BUMBU DJERUK
CHICKEN WITH LIME, JAVA STYLE

(Illustrated in black and white below)

Preparation time 5 minutes
Cooking time 40–45 minutes

You will need

4½-lb. chicken, cut in portions
scant ¼ pint (U.S. ⅔ cup) oil
1–2 cloves garlic, pounded
1 teaspoon finely chopped onion
½ teaspoon ground cumin
½ teaspoon coriander
¼ teaspoon powdered turmeric
½–1 teaspoon chilli powder
1 tablespoon soya sauce
salt and pepper
2–3 fresh limes

Trim the chicken pieces neatly and brown in oil (in a large pan). Remove. In the same pan fry garlic and onion until soft. Add cumin, coriander, turmeric, chilli powder, soya sauce and salt and pepper to taste. Mix well, cook together on low heat for 1–2 minutes. Add chicken, check seasoning and add more salt if necessary. Spoon the juices over the chicken and cook gently – about half an hour – until tender.
Squeeze the juice of 1 lime and sprinkle over the chicken. Stir, add the remaining limes cut into halves, cook for 3–4 minutes, spooning the sauce over the chicken. Serve in a deep dish with rice.

Chicken with lime, Java style

BABI KETJAP
FRIED PORK

(Illustrated in black and white on page 65)

Preparation time 5 minutes
Cooking time 20–23 minutes

You will need

1 lb. lean pork
2 tablespoons peanut oil
1 clove garlic, crushed
1 onion, finely sliced
5 tablespoons soya sauce
2 tablespoons water
1 teaspoon lemon juice
1 teaspoon brown sugar

Cut the pork into bite-sized cubes and brown in hot oil. Add garlic and onion. Fry together for 3 minutes. Blend soya sauce with water, lemon juice and sugar and pour the mixture over the pork and simmer, uncovered, for 12–15 minutes.

SAMBAL TOMAT
TOMATO SAMBAL

Preparation time 5 minutes
Cooking time 17–18 minutes

You will need

3 cloves garlic, crushed
small piece tamarind, crushed
1 small onion, chopped
2–3 tablespoons peanut oil
2 fresh red chillis, deseeded and shredded
1 lb. fresh tomatoes, peeled and sliced
1–2 well-washed leeks, sliced
salt
1 tablespoon brown sugar
¼ pint (U.S. ⅔ cup) coconut milk (see page 53)

Fry garlic, tamarind and onion in oil for 3–4 minutes. Add chillis and tomatoes. Cook, stirring, for 2 minutes. Add leeks, stir and cook for a further 2 minutes. Sprinkle with salt and sugar. Gradually blend in coconut milk, bring to the boil, simmer gently for 10 minutes and serve.

SAMBAL GORENG BUNTJIS
FRENCH BEAN SAMBAL
(Illustrated in colour on page 67)

Preparation time 8 minutes
Cooking time 16–18 minutes

You will need

1 small onion, chopped
1–2 cloves garlic
2 fresh red chillis, deseeded
small piece tamarind
2–3 tablespoons peanut oil
1 lb. French beans
1 teaspoon brown sugar
salt
1 small bay leaf
1 dried lemon leaf
½ pint (U.S. 1¼ cups) coconut milk (see page 53)

Pound together, or blend in a liquidiser, onion, garlic, chillis and tamarind until they are reduced to a smooth paste. Fry in oil for 5 minutes. Top and tail the beans, cut into 2-inch lengths and add to spice paste. Stir well. Add sugar, salt to taste, bay and lemon leaves. Gradually blend in coconut milk. Bring to the boil, then simmer uncovered for 10–12 minutes.

Note

Okra (ladies' fingers) and other vegetables can be cooked in exactly the same way, using the substitute vegetable instead of French beans.

APPLE AND MINT SAMBAL
(Illustrated in colour on the front cover)

Mix chopped raw apple with a little finely chopped mint. Dress with lemon juice, season to taste with salt and, if liked, garnish with green chillis.

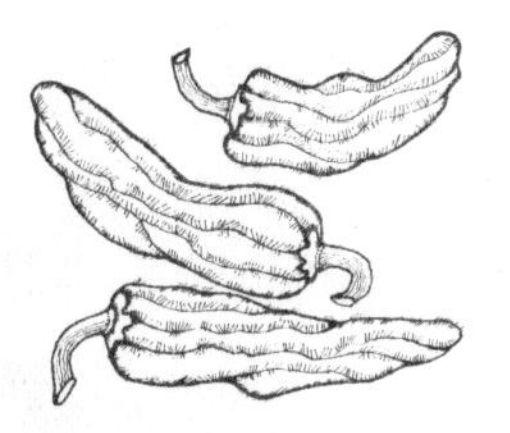

MIXED FRUIT CHUTNEY
(Illustrated in colour on the front cover)

Preparation time 5–10 minutes
Cooking time 45–50 minutes

You will need

2 lb. mixed fruit, chopped (apples, pears, peaches, plums, sultanas)
¾ pint (U.S. 2 cups) vinegar
1 lb. soft brown sugar
6–8 cloves garlic, minced
1¼ teaspoons salt
¾ teaspoon pepper or chilli powder
1 teaspoon curry powder
1 teaspoon caraway seeds

Put all prepared ingredients in an enamel pan and simmer for 45–50 minutes.
Cool, pour into clean jars; seal and store in a cool place.

SAMBAL GORENG UDANG
PRAWN SAMBAL

The Bali restaurant in Amsterdam serves this sambal with their special Rijsttafel.

Preparation time 10 minutes
Cooking time 10 minutes

You will need

1 onion, chopped
1 clove garlic, chopped
1 fresh chilli, deseeded and shredded
small piece crushed tamarind
½ bay leaf
1–2 tablespoons peanut oil
1 lb. shelled prawns
½ teaspoon ground ginger
1 teaspoon sugar
¾ pint (U.S. 2 cups) coconut milk (see page 53)

Pound the onion, garlic, chilli, tamarind and bay leaf in a mortar to make a very smooth paste. Heat oil and fry the pounded ingredients in it for 3–4 minutes; add prawns, ginger and sugar. Simmer for a few minutes, stirring constantly, then add coconut milk and blend in well. Simmer until the sauce thickens. Serve with rice.

FRIKADEL DJAGUNG
SWEET CORN

Preparation time 5 minutes
Cooking time 2 minutes

You will need

oil for deep frying
8 oz. cooked sweet corn kernels
½ stick celery, chopped
1 shallot, finely chopped
1 clove garlic, finely chopped
1 tablespoon chopped parsley
½ teaspoon salt
¼ teaspoon freshly ground pepper
1–2 eggs, beaten
1–2 tablespoons flour

Put the oil to heat. Combine rest of ingredients and taking a spoonful at a time drop into hot oil. Fry until crisp and golden.

DADAR IRIS
SHREDDED OMELETTE

Preparation time 5 minutes
Cooking time 15–16 minutes

You will need

1–2 tablespoons butter or oil
3–4 spring onions, chopped
1 tomato, peeled and chopped
4 oz. ham, cut in thin strips
pinch salt
pinch chilli powder
3–4 tablespoons soya sauce
4 eggs

Heat the butter or oil and fry the onions until soft. Add tomato and cook together for 2–3 minutes. Add ham, season with salt, chilli powder and half the soya sauce. Cook for 3 minutes. Beat the eggs and stir into the pan, cover, lower heat to minimum and cook until done. Remove omelette, shred finely, sprinkle with remaining soya sauce and serve.

Rijsttafel (see recipes pages 56–66)

Fried pork (see recipe page 62)

SERUNDENG
SPICED COCONUT

This is a coconut condiment, a small helping of which is served with Rijsttafel, along with dishes of various atjar or vegetable pickles.

Preparation time 10 minutes
Cooking time 5–6 minutes

You will need

1 onion, chopped
1–2 cloves garlic, crushed
1-inch piece root ginger, chopped
1 small bay leaf
1 teaspoon coriander
½ teaspoon cumin
8 oz. shredded coconut
2–3 tablespoons water
salt
1 teaspoon soft brown sugar
4 oz. peanuts, lightly roasted

Pound together or blend in a liquidiser the onion, garlic, ginger, bay leaf, coriander and cumin. Quickly dry-fry (i.e. without any fat) this spice paste to brown lightly.
In a separate pan, dry-fry coconut, to brown lightly. Add spice paste and the water, season with salt to taste, sprinkle with the sugar and cook together for 3–4 minutes. Stir in peanuts and serve.

SAMBAL GORENG TELUR
SPICED EGGS

Preparation time 25 minutes
Cooking time 25–30 minutes

You will need

4 eggs
1½ tablespoons chopped onion
1 clove garlic, chopped
1 tablespoon grated fresh ginger
1 teaspoon cumin
1 teaspoon coriander
2 tablespoons peanut oil
½ pint (U.S. 1¼ cups) coconut milk (see page 53)

Put the eggs into enough cold water to cover, bring to the boil. As soon as boiling is established, cover the pan, turn off heat and leave for 15 minutes. Dip in cold water, shell and cut in half. Pound the onion, garlic, ginger, cumin and coriander into a smooth mixture (or blend in a liquidiser). Heat the oil and fry the pounded spices for 5–6 minutes stirring all the time. Add coconut milk gradually, then the eggs, simmer gently without a lid for 10–12 minutes and serve.

SAMBAL GORENG IKAN
FISH SAMBAL

Preparation time 20 minutes
Cooking time 9–11 minutes

You will need

3 cloves garlic
2 fresh red chillis, deseeded, *or* 1 teaspoon chilli powder
½ teaspoon cumin seed
¼ teaspoon turmeric
2–3 tablespoons peanut oil
1 green sweet pepper, deseeded and sliced
1 large onion, finely sliced
1-inch piece root ginger, finely chopped
1 lb. fish (any firm white fish), boiled, skinned and boned
salt
½ pint (U.S. 1¼ cups) coconut milk (see page 53)

Pound together in a mortar or blend in a liquidiser the garlic, chillis, cumin and turmeric until they form a smooth paste. Heat oil and fry green pepper, onion and ginger for 2 minutes. Then stir in spice paste quickly. Add fish, which should have been lightly boiled (not overcooked) and cut into portions. Gently cook the fish for 2–3 minutes so that it absorbs the spice flavours. Season to taste with salt. Add coconut milk and simmer for 5–6 minutes.

SAMBAL GORENG HATI AJAM
CHICKEN LIVER SAMBAL (1)

Preparation time 10 minutes
Cooking time 20 minutes

You will need

1 chopped onion
1 clove garlic
½ teaspoon tamarind (in a piece, if possible)
1–2 fresh chillis, deseeded
2–3 tablespoons peanut oil
1 lb. chicken livers
½ teaspoon ground ginger
1 teaspoon brown sugar
salt
generous ½ pint (U.S. 1½ cups) coconut milk (see page 53)

Pound together, or blend in a liquidiser to a smooth paste, the onion, garlic, tamarind and chillis. Fry in oil for 5 minutes. Cut livers into bite-sized pieces, add to fried spices, sprinkle with ginger and sugar, season with salt to taste and fry lightly stirring all the time to mix well. Add coconut milk, blending it in a little at a time. Simmer until the sauce thickens. Serve with boiled rice.

SAMBAL HATI AJAM
CHICKEN LIVER SAMBAL (2)

Preparation time 10 minutes
Cooking time 20–22 minutes

You will need

liver and giblets from one chicken
1½ oz. chopped onion
1 tablespoon sliced fresh ginger
3–4 red chillis, deseeded
3–4 cloves garlic, chopped
1–2 tablespoons peanut oil
1 teaspoon salt
1 teaspoon sugar
1 tablespoon tamarind pulp
1 pint (U.S. 2½ cups) coconut milk (see page 53)

Chop the liver and the giblets.
Pound in a mortar the onion, ginger, chillis and garlic, then fry in hot oil for 3–4 minutes, stirring constantly.
Add liver and giblets, brown well, add salt and sugar and cook gently until done.
Blend tamarind with coconut milk, add to pan and simmer, stirring all the time, until the sauce thickens.

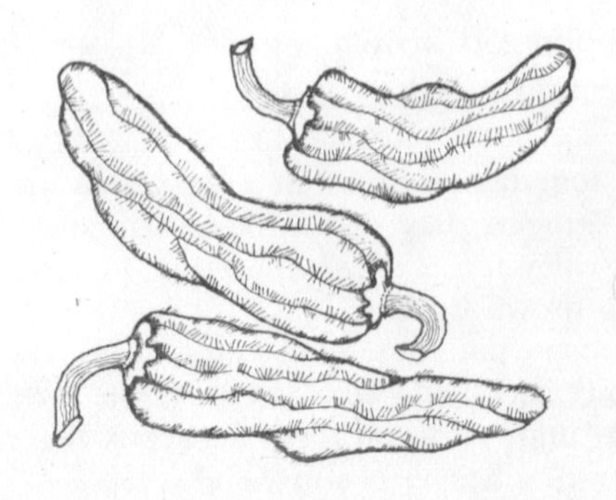

Selection of sambals (see recipes pages 62–63)

Christmas ham (see recipe page 74)

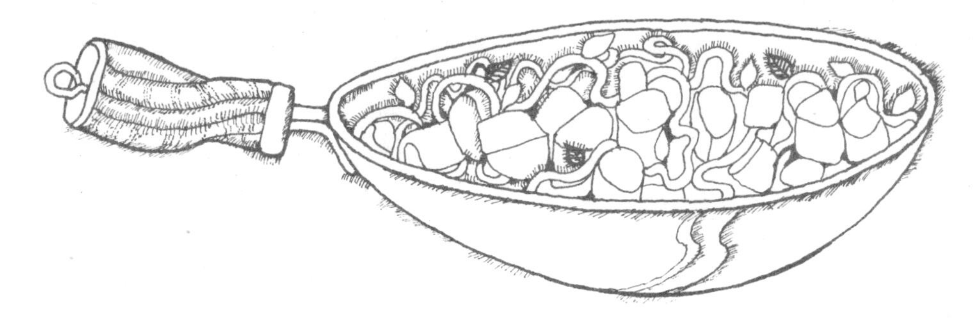

PHILIPPINES

The distinction of cooking in the Philippines is the strong Spanish influence due to 400 years of Spanish rule. Except for the use of some local exotic produce, the menu of a Manila restaurant can read like that of a Spanish eating place. For instance, one restaurant offers as a local speciality a somewhat simplified version of Arroz a la Valenciana. Sucking pigs, cooked in the approved Spanish manner (see page 73), are served at village fiestas.

LUMPIANG UBOD
STUFFED PANCAKES WITH PALM HEARTS

(Illustrated in black and white on page 71)

This is a speciality of the Philippines, a variation of the pancake roll. The ingredient which gives the dish its name, ubod, is coconut palm heart, available in jars from delicatessen. A combination of equal amounts of bean sprouts and spring onions may be used as a substitute.
The lumpia batter is made with egg and cornflour and the Lumpiang Ubod is served with a garlic-flavoured, sweetened soya sauce.

Preparation time 30 minutes
Cooking time 8–10 minutes
To serve 4–6

To make the filling

2 tablespoons oil
1 clove garlic, chopped
1 small onion, thinly sliced
4 oz. parboiled lean pork, diced
2 oz. ham, shredded
4 tablespoons peeled chopped prawns
2 oz. cooked chick peas (optional)
8 oz. ubod (coconut palm hearts), shredded
6 oz. French beans, shredded
1 carrot, shredded
12 oz. cabbage, shredded
salt and pepper
12 spring onions
12 crisp lettuce leaves
12 lumpia (pancakes) (see page 70)
lumpiang ubod sauce (see page 70)

Heat the oil and lightly fry garlic and onion until soft. Add pork and ham and cook, stirring, for 2 minutes. Add prawns and chick peas and cook for a further 2 minutes.
Stir in the ubod, beans, carrot and cabbage. Season with salt and pepper, cover and simmer until the vegetables are just cooked. They must remain firm and crisp.
Drain and allow to cool.
Wrap a portion of the lumpiang ubod filling and a long spring onion first in a lettuce leaf, then in a pancake. Arrange on a wooden serving platter and serve with lumpiang ubod sauce.

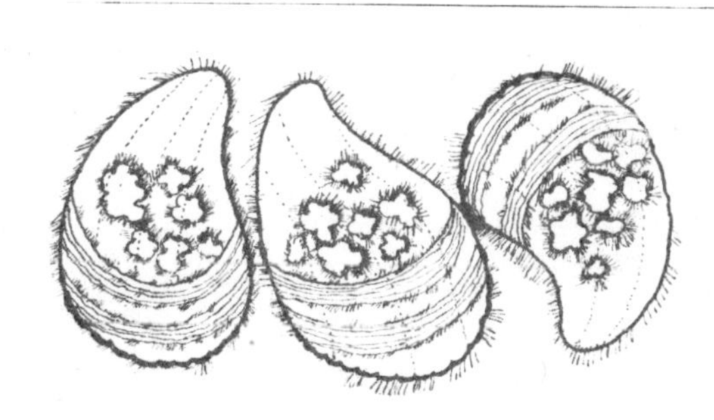

LUMPIA
PANCAKES

Preparation time 3 minutes
Cooking time 8 minutes
To make 12 pancakes

You will need

2 eggs
3 oz. cornflour
$\frac{1}{2}$ pint (U.S. $1\frac{1}{4}$ cups) water
peanut oil

Separate the eggs and whisk the whites until very stiff, and fold in lightly beaten yolks. Blend the cornflour with water, adding the water gradually to ensure smoothness. Stir thoroughly into the egg.
Lightly brush the frying pan with oil and heat. Using 2 tablespoons of the lumpia batter at a time, fry very thin pancakes. Tilt the pan to spread the batter evenly, do not turn and do not allow the pancakes to colour. Remove and keep warm until the whole batch is cooked.

LUMPIANG UBOD SAUCE
STUFFED PANCAKE SAUCE

Preparation time 5 minutes
Cooking time 5–6 minutes

You will need

generous $\frac{1}{4}$ pint (U.S. $\frac{3}{4}$ cup) stock (or water with a stock cube)
2 oz. sugar
2 tablespoons dark soya sauce
1 teaspoon salt
1 tablespoon cornflour
3 tablespoons cold water
1–2 teaspoons finely minced garlic

Bring the stock to the boil with the sugar, soya sauce and salt. If you are using a stock cube, make allowances for its high salt content.
Blend the cornflour with the cold water, adding the water a little at a time, to prevent formation of lumps. Stir the cornflour liquid into the stock. Simmer, stirring, for 2–3 minutes, until the sauce thickens.
Pour into a serving dish, a wooden one for preference, sprinkle the garlic on to it, and serve with lumpiang ubod (see page 69).

ENSALADA ITLOG
EGG SALAD

Preparation time 10 minutes plus chilling time
Cooking time nil
To serve 4

You will need

4 hard-boiled eggs
1 large, hot cooked potato, mashed
1 cup hot, cooked rice
$\frac{1}{4}$ pint (U.S. $\frac{2}{3}$ cup) French dressing (see page 126)
2 tablespoons chopped sweet pepper
1 tablespoon finely chopped onion
1 tablespoon chopped parsley
salt and pepper

Shell eggs and rub 2 of them through a sieve; mix with the potato and rice. Stir in the French dressing and chill. Add sweet pepper, onion and parsley. Mix well and add salt and pepper to taste.
Rub remaining eggs through a sieve, sprinkle over salad and serve.

SCALLOPS NA MAY KALAMANSI
SCALLOPS IN LIME JUICE
(Fresh scallops illustrated in colour on page 30)

Preparation time	7 minutes plus 7–8 hours chilling time
Cooking time	nil
To serve	4

You will need

12 whole scallops
1 onion, thinly sliced
dash white wine vinegar
salt
cayenne pepper
$\frac{1}{4}$ pint (U.S. $\frac{2}{3}$ cup) lime juice

Wash and drain scallops. Cut into thin round slices. Put in a salad bowl.
Cover with the onion, add vinegar, season to taste with salt and cayenne pepper. Sprinkle on the lime juice. Chill for 7–8 hours.
Serve with hot toast.

PESCADO A LA ILO-ILO
HALIBUT, ILO-ILO STYLE

Preparation time	3 minutes plus 1 hour marinating
Cooking time	nil
To serve	4

You will need

1 lb. halibut
1 teaspoon salt
$\frac{1}{2}$ pint (U.S. $1\frac{1}{4}$ cups) water
juice of 3 limes *or* lemons
1 teaspoon white rum

Wash the halibut, dry, and cut into bite-sized pieces and place in a dish. Add salt to water and mix well; pour over the fish and leave for 1 hour. Drain, rinse and drain again thoroughly. Arrange halibut in a serving dish, pour lime juice over, sprinkle with rum and serve.

Stuffed pancakes with palm hearts (see recipe page 69)

BAPA NG MAY SAGING
SOLE WITH BANANAS
(Illustrated in black and white below)

Preparation time 3 minutes
Cooking time 7 minutes
To serve 6

You will need

6 sole fillets
salt and pepper
½ lemon
1 egg, beaten
breadcrumbs
3 oz. butter
3 firm bananas
parsley

Wash and dry the fillets, season with salt and pepper, squeeze a few drops of lemon juice on each. Dip in the beaten egg and then in the breadcrumbs. Heat the butter and fry the fillets until golden on both sides, drain and keep hot. Peel bananas, cut in half lengthways, sprinkle with lemon juice and fry in butter, just to soften the fruit. Do not overcook or they will become mis-shapen and difficult to handle. Put half a banana on each sole fillet and serve immediately sprinkled with parsley.
Any flat fish such as plaice, dab or brill can be used instead of sole.

Note
Instead of using fillets and frying in breadcrumbs, grill the seasoned fish whole and serve with sliced bananas.

Sole with bananas

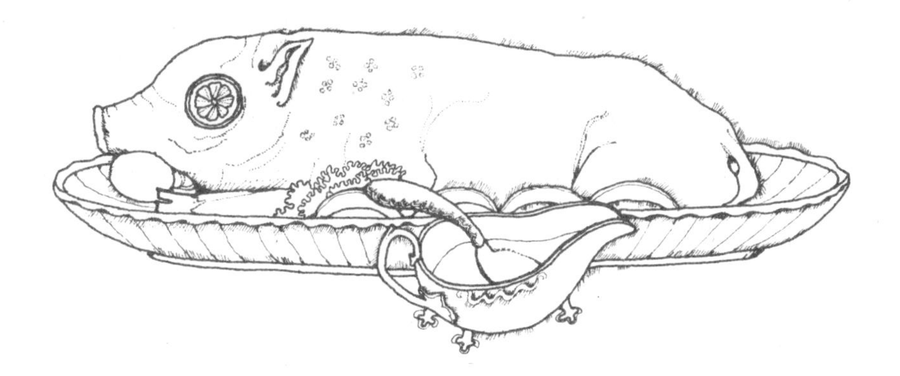

LECHON
ROAST SUCKING PIG

Preparation time 5 minutes
Cooking time 35 minutes per pound of meat
To serve 8
Oven temperature 191°C., 375°F., Gas Mark 5

You will need

1 sucking pig and its liver
salt and pepper
12 tamarind leaves *or* lemon slices
melted lard *or* oil
½ pint (U.S. 1¼ cups) boiling water
5–6 cloves garlic, finely chopped
2–3 medium onions, sliced
3 tablespoons lime juice *or* vinegar
1–2 tablespoons sugar

Get your butcher to prepare the sucking pig for roasting. Reserve the liver, which is to be used in the sauce.
Rub the inside of the sucking pig with a mixture of salt and pepper, put the tamarind leaves or lemon slices inside, and brush the outside liberally with lard or oil.
Roast on a spit, or on a grid in the oven pre-heated to the temperature given above allowing 35 minutes per pound. Protect the ears with oiled greaseproof paper or foil and baste the sucking pig frequently with the pan juices. Meanwhile, make the sauce. Slice the liver, brown lightly in 2 tablespoons lard, then chop or mince. Add the boiling water and rub the mixture through a fine sieve or put through a blender.
Heat 2 tablespoons lard or oil and brown the garlic. Remove and keep on a dish. In the same fat fry the onions until soft, but do not allow them to colour.
Add liver sauce to onions, sprinkle with lime juice or vinegar and sugar, and season to taste. Simmer very slowly, stirring all the time.
Pour the sauce into a heated sauceboat, sprinkle garlic on top and serve with the roast sucking pig.

DU MALAGANG MANOK
SPRING CHICKEN, MANILA STYLE

Preparation time 2 minutes
Cooking time 20–25 minutes
To serve 4

You will need

4 pints (U.S. 10 cups) water
1 oz. fresh ginger, minced
2 teaspoons sugar
1¾ pints (U.S. 4¼ cups) pineapple juice
salt
4 poussins (young chickens)
oil for deep frying
4 oz. peanut butter
generous ¼ pint (U.S. ¾ cup) chicken stock
1 teaspoon Worcestershire sauce
few drops Tabasco

Put the water in a pan deep enough to take all ingredients. Add the ginger, sugar, pineapple juice and 1 tablespoon salt. Bring to the boil.
Add the poussins, simmer for 7–10 minutes or until tender. Drain, dry on a cloth and cool.
Heat the oil and deep-fry the poussins. Drain and arrange on a serving dish.
Heat the peanut butter slowly. Stir in the stock, Worcestershire sauce and Tabasco. Season with salt to taste. Bring sauce to simmering point and pour into a dish. Serve as a dip with the poussins.

PATO NG MAY TSOKOLATE
CHOCOLATE DUCK

Preparation time 3 minutes
Cooking time 1 hour 35 minutes – 1 hour 45 minutes
To serve 4

You will need

4 tablespoons oil
5-lb. duck, dressed
1 teaspoon wine vinegar
3 tablespoons sherry
juice of 1 lime *or* lemon
1 bay leaf
2 sprigs parsley
2 carrots, thinly sliced
2 oz. bitter cooking chocolate, grated
$\frac{1}{4}$ pint (U.S. $\frac{2}{3}$ cup) stock
salt and pepper
8–12 chipolata sausages (optional)

Heat the oil in a large pan and brown the duck on all sides.
Add the rest of the ingredients, except the sausages, cover with a well-fitting lid and cook over a low heat for 1 hour.
Put in the sausages, if used, and continue to cook for another 25–30 minutes, until the duck is tender.
Serve with boiled rice.

JAMÓN DE NAVIDAD
CHRISTMAS HAM
(Illustrated in colour on page 68)

Preparation time 5 minutes
Cooking time 2 hours – 2 hours 45 minutes
To serve 12–16
Oven temperature 218°C., 425°F., Gas Mark 7

You will need

1 boned, smoked ham (6–8 lb.)
generous $\frac{1}{2}$ pint (U.S. $1\frac{1}{2}$ cups) pineapple juice
1 pint (U.S. $2\frac{1}{2}$ cups) beer
5–6 cloves
1-inch stick cinnamon
pinch oregano
1 bay leaf
small pinch thyme
brown sugar for glazing

FOR GARNISH
pineapple rings
glacé cherries

Put the ham in a pan with enough cold water to cover, slowly bring to the boil, and cook for 25–30 minutes. Discard the liquid (it will not have absorbed enough flavour, and will be too salty, for use as stock).
Skin the ham. Put it back in the pan with the rest of the ingredients, except sugar, pineapple rings and cherries. Bring to the boil and simmer until cooked – allowing about 15 minutes to the pound. Turn on oven to temperature given, for about 15 minutes before ham is cooked.
Drain ham, place in a roasting pan, sprinkle generously with brown sugar and heat in the oven until the sugar melts to give a glaze (5–15 minutes).
Serve in thin slices garnished with pineapple rings and glacé cherries.

A PAY NG BAKA
CALVES' LIVER

Preparation time 20 minutes
Cooking time 13–15 minutes
To serve 4

You will need

1 lb. calves' liver
1 onion, sliced
1 clove garlic
1 fresh chilli *or* a pinch of chilli powder
1 teaspoon lime *or* lemon juice
2 tablespoons peanut oil
$\frac{1}{2}$ teaspoon ground ginger
1 teaspoon brown sugar
$\frac{1}{2}$ pint (U.S. $1\frac{1}{4}$ cups) coconut milk (see page 53)

Cut the liver into bite-sized pieces. Put the onion, garlic, and chilli into a mortar, moisten with lime or lemon juice, and pound into a smooth paste.
Heat the oil and fry the pounded mixture for 6–7 minutes, stirring all the time. Add liver, sprinkle with ginger and brown sugar, and cook for 2–3 minutes. Add coconut milk, simmer for 5 minutes, and serve.

ADOBONG MANOK AT BABOY

PORK AND CHICKEN EN ADOBO

Preparation time 15 minutes plus 15 minutes standing time
Cooking time 25 minutes
To serve 6

You will need

1 lb. lean pork, cut in 2-inch cubes
$2\frac{1}{2}$-lb. chicken, cut in small pieces
5 cloves garlic, finely chopped
2–3 small bay leaves
4 tablespoons (U.S. $\frac{1}{3}$ cup) vinegar
salt and pepper
boiling water
2 tablespoons butter or oil, if needed
$\frac{1}{2}$ pint (U.S. $1\frac{1}{4}$ cups) coconut cream (see page 53)

Place the pork and chicken in a casserole, with the garlic, bay leaves, vinegar, salt and pepper. Leave to stand for 15 minutes, stirring from time to time, to impregnate the meat with the seasoning. Add just enough boiling water to cover the ingredients, cover, and simmer until the water evaporates. If the pork does not render sufficient fat, add butter or oil and continue to cook until the pork and the chicken are uniformly brown on all sides. When cooked, gently heat the coconut cream and stir into the casserole. Serve with boiled rice. This kind of braising is a favourite method of cooking in the Philippines and is applied to fish, meat and poultry.

CARNE CON ARROZ Y PLÁTANOS

MINCED MEAT WITH RICE AND BANANAS

Preparation time 5 minutes
Cooking time 20–25 minutes
To serve 4–5

This is an appetising way to use up meat left-overs, and makes an interesting change from shepherd's pie.

You will need

8 oz. rice
1 pint (U.S. $2\frac{1}{2}$ cups) water
small pinch saffron
2 medium onions
$1\frac{1}{2}$ tablespoons oil
1 lb. cooked meat, minced
salt and pepper
4–5 bananas, peeled
tomato sauce (see page 76)
4–5 eggs (optional)

Put the rice in a pan with the water and saffron, and cook by any of the Chinese ways described on page 80.
Meanwhile chop the onions, and fry in the oil until soft and transparent. Add the meat, season to taste, and cook for 5–6 minutes. Remove and keep hot. Cut the bananas in half lengthways, and fry lightly in remaining oil.
Make a border of rice on a serving dish. Pile the meat in the middle, and garnish with the bananas. Decorate with tomato sauce and serve piping hot.
If a more substantial dish is required, fry the eggs and place these on the dish.

SALSA DE TOMATE
TOMATO SAUCE

Preparation time 12 minutes
Cooking time 20 minutes
To serve 4

You will need

1 lb. tomatoes, peeled and quartered
2 oz. dried shrimps, pounded
4 medium onions, sliced
2 cloves garlic, chopped
pinch turmeric
pinch salt
3 tablespoons oil
3 tablespoons water

Put all ingredients into a pan in the order in which they are listed, bring to the boil, then simmer until the onions are tender and the liquid almost evaporated.

ENSALADA PAW PAW
PAW-PAW SALAD

Preparation time 15 minutes plus 1 hour chilling
Cooking time nil
To serve 4–6

You will need

2 paw-paws, peeled and deseeded
4 passion fruit
2 sweet oranges, peeled and sliced
4 slices pineapple, cut in pieces
$\frac{1}{4}$ pint (U.S. $\frac{2}{3}$ cup) pineapple juice
1 tablespoon white rum

Dice paw-paws and scoop out the pulp from the passion fruit. Arrange all fruit in a bowl with pineapple as garnish. Pour pineapple juice over the salad and sprinkle with rum. Chill and serve.

Bean curd with prawns (see recipe page 95)

Cold hors d'oeuvre (see recipe page 82)

CHINA

China is the cradle of one of the great cuisines, and like Chinese art and literature, its cooking has a distinct personality.
The Chinese are fastidious about their food and it is recorded that Confucius, twenty-five centuries ago, lectured against eating 'anything over-cooked, under-cooked, untidily cut or deficient in seasoning'.
Chinese delicacies are innumerable. Each province has contributed a great number of specialities to the national repertoire.
The Chinese custom of cutting up all the food in the kitchen and using seasoning during cooking makes unnecessary the display on the dinner table of such savage implements as knives, and the eaters need not start sprinkling food with seasoning which it won't have time to absorb. As the food is served in convenient bite-sized pieces, chopsticks are ideal for eating it, and that is why many other countries in the Far East have adopted them.
Chopsticks are easy to manipulate with practice. They enable one to hold the right amount of sauce each morsel requires to preserve the subtle interchange of flavours, and the difference their use makes to the enjoyment of food is tremendous.
The Chinese seldom serve desserts or sweets, except in the north, where the cold climate warrants it. This could account for the fact that Chinese people often look twenty years younger than their age, keep their teeth and the women preserve a youthful line long past middle age!

RICE COOKING IN CHINA

Rice, the staple food of the Chinese, occupies roughly the same place in the Chinese diet as, say, bread does in the French diet. The appearance of cooked rice is considered to be of great importance. If cooked correctly – and this is mainly a question of observing the right proportions of rice to water – the grains should be firm and separate. Rice should be washed thoroughly before cooking (our cook in China used to say 'in nine waters') and the last water poured off should be completely clear.

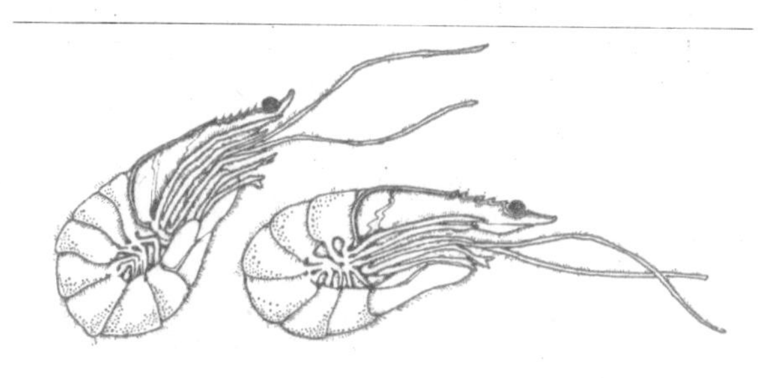

CHOW FAN
FRIED RICE

Preparation time 3 minutes
Cooking time 7–8 minutes
To serve 6–8

You will need

1 tablespoon lard or oil
1 lb. cooked rice
4 oz. cooked, peeled prawns
2 eggs, beaten
3–4 spring onions, chopped
1 tablespoon soya sauce

Heat the lard or oil in pan. Fry the rice quickly stirring all the time. Stir in prawns. Pour eggs over rice, fry slowly for 4–5 minutes. Sprinkle with spring onions, season with soya sauce and serve.

BARK FAN
BOILED RICE (1)

Preparation time 5 minutes
Cooking time 23 minutes
To serve 6–8

You will need

1 lb. rice
1½ pints (U.S. 3¾ cups) water

Wash the rice thoroughly until the water is clear. Put the rice and water in a thick saucepan, bring to the boil and cover as soon as boiling is established. Leave to simmer undisturbed for 20 minutes.

BARK FAN
BOILED RICE (2)

Preparation time 5 minutes
Cooking time 17 minutes
To serve 3–4

You will need

8 oz. rice
water

Wash the rice thoroughly until the water is clear. Put the rice into a fairly wide saucepan and cover with water, allowing 'two fingers' i.e. 1 inch of water above the level of the rice. Bring to the boil and allow to boil fast until the water is absorbed. Cover with a lid, reduce heat to the minimum and leave for 12 minutes.

BARK FAN
BOILED RICE (3)

Preparation time 5 minutes
Cooking time 17 minutes
To serve 3–4

You will need

8 oz. rice
generous ¾ pint (U.S. 2 cups) water

Wash the rice several times. Add water, bring to the boil, cover and boil quickly until the water evaporates. Do not stir while rice is boiling, as this will prevent the grains from separating.
Keep warm until ready for use, leaving the lid on. (If an electric cooker is used, heat may be turned off and the pot kept covered on the hotplate. If the rice is cooked on a gas cooker, turn the flame down very low after the water has evaporated.)

BARK BOW FAN
MOST PRECIOUS RICE

Preparation time 15 minutes
Cooking time 12 minutes
To serve 8

You will need

8 oz. lean pork or chicken
4 oz. peeled prawns or crab meat
8 oz. shelled peas or green beans – topped, tailed and sliced
4 oz. mushrooms, sliced
1–2 tablespoons spring onions, chopped
2–3 eggs
2 teaspoons soya sauce
oil
salt and pepper
1½–2 lb. cold cooked rice

Cut meat, fish and vegetables uniformly, determining the size and shape by the smallest natural ingredient; thus, if peas are used, the rest of the ingredients must be cut into dice no bigger than a pea.
Beat eggs with soya sauce and reserve. Cook all the diced ingredients in a deep, oiled pan, season to taste with salt and pepper and add the rice, stirring until it becomes quite hot and the rice grains separate. Pour the eggs over the whole mixture.
Increase heat to cook quickly and keep stirring until the eggs have been integrated into the mixture and are quite dry.

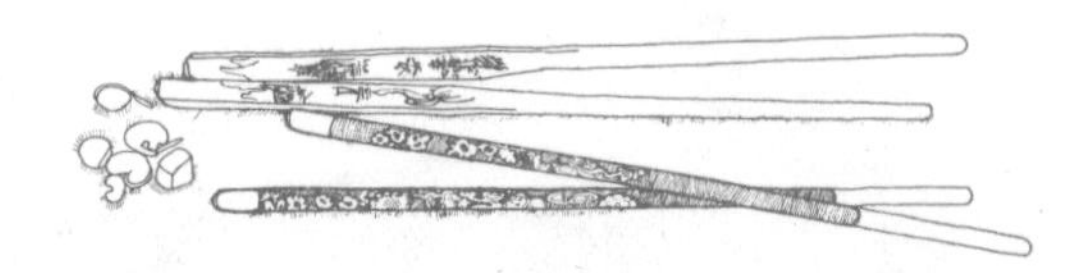

NOODLES

DAN MIEN
HOME-MADE NOODLES

Preparation time 10 minutes
Cooking time 5 minutes
To serve 4

You will need

1 lb. flour
½ teaspoon salt
2 eggs

Make a dough, using 12 oz. flour, the salt and eggs. Knead well and roll out thinly. (To ensure evenness of rolling out, always roll forward.) Use the rest of the flour for sprinkling the pastry board to prevent sticking. Fold the dough and cut into strips – narrow ones for soup, wider ones for braising or frying. Sprinkle a little flour over the strips and separate them on the board. (If not using immediately, cover with a damp cloth.) Allow 3 pints (U.S. 7½ cups) water to boil 1 lb. noodles. Always put the noodles into boiling water, separating them with a pair of chopsticks to prevent sticking. Boil for 5 minutes and drain.

KAI SEE JAR MIEN
CRISPY NOODLES WITH CHICKEN AND BAMBOO SHOOTS

Preparation time 6 minutes
Cooking time 14 minutes
To serve 4

You will need

1 lb. home-made Chinese noodles (see above)
1 lb. lard for deep frying
1–2 tablespoons peanut oil
4 oz. uncooked chicken meat, diced
salt and pepper
2 oz. bamboo shoots, sliced
3 oz. bean sprouts
2 oz. mushrooms, sliced
1 medium onion, chopped
1 teaspoon cornflour
2 tablespoons cold water
2 teaspoons soya sauce
few drops sesame oil

Boil the noodles for 5 minutes, rinse under running cold water and drain well.
Heat the lard. Arrange the noodles in a strainer or frying basket and deep-fry for 5 minutes, by which time they should be crispy and golden. Press the noodles to sides of frying basket to form a 'nest'. Take the basket out of the fat and shake to allow surplus fat to drip off. Transfer noodle nest to a heated serving dish and keep hot.
Heat the peanut oil and cook the chicken for 1 minute. Season with salt and pepper to taste. Add bamboo shoots, bean sprouts, mushrooms and onion. Cook together for 1 minute, stirring all the time.
Blend the cornflour with the water and soya sauce, stir into the pan and cook for a further minute. Sprinkle with sesame oil and serve the mixture on top of the noodles.

CHOW MAI
RICE NOODLES

Preparation time 10 minutes plus 30 minutes standing time
Cooking time 5 minutes
To serve 2

You will need

6 oz. thick rice noodles
1 tablespoon oil
8 oz. lobster meat, diced
3 oz. bean sprouts
4 fresh mushrooms, sliced
2 oz. cucumber, sliced
2 oz. water chestnuts, sliced
2 oz. bamboo shoots, sliced
1 stick celery, sliced
¼ medium onion, sliced
½ teaspoon salt
1 teaspoon sugar
2 teaspoons soya sauce
stock

Put the noodles in a bowl, cover with hot water and leave to stand for 30 minutes. Heat oil in a pan and sauté the lobster for 1 minute. Add all the vegetables and cook together for 1 minute. Add salt, sugar, soya sauce and enough stock to cover. Cook for 1 minute, add drained noodles, cook for a further 2 minutes and serve.

MIEN
CHINESE NOODLE OR WUN TUN PASTE

This dough is used for Chinese noodles, wun tun and various other patties and dumplings.

Preparation time 10 minutes
To serve 4–6

You will need

1 lb. plain flour
2 eggs
water

Mix flour and eggs and add enough water to make a pliable dough. Roll out paper-thin then, if used for Chinese noodles, fold over 6–8 times, dusting the layers with plain flour, and cut into strips $\frac{1}{8}$ inch wide. If using for wun tun or patties, cut into 2-inch squares. Cook as required.

WUN TUN
DUMPLINGS

Preparation time 15 minutes
Cooking time 7 minutes
To serve 6

You will need

1½ lb. lean pork
salt
1 oz. dried mushrooms
6 oz. shelled prawns
½ teaspoon monosodium glutamate (optional)
4 oz. spring onions, chopped
2 teaspoons cornflour
2 teaspoons soya sauce
1 teaspoon brandy
1 teaspoon oil
2 eggs
wun tun paste (see above)

Mince the pork and season with salt to taste. Scald and shred the mushrooms. Combine pork, mushrooms, prawns, monosodium glutamate, 3 oz. of the spring onions, cornflour, soya sauce, brandy, oil and 1 egg. Blend well. Beat second egg and reserve.

Roll out the paste and cut into 2-inch squares. Place a teaspoon of the pork mixture on each square. Fold paste over, seal with beaten egg and round off edges. Cook for 7 minutes in plenty of fast-boiling water, with the pan uncovered. Drain, sprinkle with remaining spring onions and use as required. Serve in a clear stock, by themselves or with noodles.

HORS D'OEUVRE AND SOUPS

TUNG FOON
COLD HORS D'OEUVRE
(Illustrated in colour on page 78)

The Chinese have a splendid way of presenting assorted cold foods. The selection of the food to be served on one dish (see a typical assortment on page 78) can be varied according to individual taste and the ingredients available.
The selection shown includes chicken, beef, liver, canned abalone or awabi, and ham. Fried chicken (page 101) is particularly suitable for serving as a cold hors d'oeuvre. So are braised mushrooms, omelette and all vegetables which retain their firmness and therefore lend themselves to being shaped into attractive patterns.
The presentation I have chosen is one of the simplest, but it requires accurate slicing. The slices must be thin and uniform so that each component of the assortment can be arranged in the desired pattern. In the illustration each kind of food forms one petal of a flower. Alternatively, the ham, chicken, liver or whatever you are using, can be sliced into petal shapes and then assembled into individual flowers.
Strips of omelette can be made into daisies or chrysanthemums.

Winter melon soup

HAR BENG
PRAWN CRACKERS

Preparation time nil
Cooking time 1 minute
To serve 4

You will need

peanut oil for deep frying
4-oz. can prawn crackers

Heat the oil, drop into it a few cracker pellets at a time. As soon as they puff up and float to the surface (this takes only a few seconds) take them out with a perforated spoon and drain on absorbent paper.
Do not let the crackers turn colour or they will be spoiled, so take care not to overheat the oil.

TUNG KWAH CHUK
WINTER MELON SOUP

(Illustrated in colour on page 88 and black and white below)

This dish is both delicious and decorative. Chinese cooks often turn a winter melon into a veritable work of art by intricate carving, decorating it with attractive designs, or etching it with appropriate messages.

Preparation time 15 minutes
Cooking time 1 hour 45 minutes – 2 hours
To serve 4

You will need

1 oz. dried mushrooms
4 oz. bamboo shoots
4 oz. lean ham or bacon
4–5 lb. winter melon
8 oz. uncooked chicken, shredded
8 oz. uncooked pork, shredded
pinch monosodium glutamate (optional)
1 knob green ginger
2½ pints (U.S. 6 cups) water
salt and pepper

Blanch the mushrooms and cut into thin strips. Dice the bamboo shoots and cut ham into shreds. Cut the top off the melon and scoop out some pulp evenly, to enlarge the cavity, which is to serve as a saucepan. Keep the top to use as a lid.
Put the chicken, pork, monosodium glutamate, ginger, mushrooms and bamboo shoots in a pan with the water. Add bones from chicken or pork wrapped in a muslin bag. Bring to the boil, skim, then simmer on very low heat for 40 minutes. Remove and discard bones. Season to taste.
Stand the melon in a large pudding basin to keep it firmly upright. Pour the soup into it, add ham and replace top.
Steam for 1 hour–1 hour 15 minutes, until the melon is cooked.
The soup is served in the melon, some of the melon flesh being scooped out for each serving.

YIN WOR TONG
BIRDS' NEST SOUP

Preparation time 10 minutes plus 4 hours soaking time
Cooking time 2 hours 15 minutes
To serve 6

You will need

4 oz. birds' nest
4 pints (U.S. 10 cups) chicken stock
1 leg of chicken
2 teaspoons water-chestnut flour
1–2 tablespoons water
salt and pepper
1 egg white
2 oz. cooked chicken, chopped
1 oz. ham, finely chopped
2 oz. fresh mushrooms, chopped
3 spring onions, chopped

Soak the birds' nest in hot water for 4 hours. Drain and simmer in the chicken stock for 10 minutes. Transfer to a fireproof dish, put in top of steamer, place chicken leg on top, cover and steam for 2 hours.
Remove chicken leg and any water that may have dropped on the birds' nest from the lid.
Mix water-chestnut flour with water to a smooth paste. Place birds' nest in saucepan, cover with stock, bring to boil, season with salt and pepper and stir in water-chestnut paste.
Simmer for 2 minutes, stirring all the time. Add egg white and, when soup becomes semi-transparent, garnish with chopped chicken, ham, mushrooms and spring onions. Serve hot.

KAM NING TONG
SILVER AND GOLD SOUP
(Illustrated in colour on page 89)

Prepare clear chicken stock, season to taste. Allow 2–4 pigeon eggs per portion. Carefully poach half the eggs, or, better still, break them into individual, lightly greased, soya sauce dishes and steam until set, but do not over-cook. The yolks of the poached or steamed eggs will have a film of white over them, giving them the 'silver' appearance.
Gently fry the rest of the eggs, taking care not to break the yolks – for these supply the 'gold' element.
Serve the soup in individual bowls with 1 or 2 silver eggs and 1 or 2 gold eggs floating in each.

HIEN TZU AAP TONG
LOTUS SEED AND DUCK SOUP

Preparation time 22 minutes
Cooking time 2 hours 5 minutes
To serve 6–8

You will need

2½-lb. duck
3½ pints (U.S. 9 cups) water plus ¼ pint (U.S. ⅔ cup) water
2 oz. bamboo shoots
2 oz. fresh mushrooms
1 oz. water chestnuts
1 teaspoon cornflour
2 teaspoons sherry
small can fresh lotus seeds
1 teaspoon sesame oil
1 teaspoon soya sauce
salt and pepper

Bone the duck. Simmer bones in 3½ pints water for 2 hours.
Meanwhile slice meat finely and reserve. Shred bamboo shoots, mushrooms and water chestnuts and mix together.
Blend cornflour with the ¼ pint water, add sherry and pour over duck.
Strain stock, and return it to the pan; add mushroom mixture, lotus seeds and duck mixture. Simmer 3 minutes; stir in sesame oil and soya sauce. Season with salt and pepper and serve.

MOW GOO KAI PIN TONG
CHICKEN AND MUSHROOM SOUP

Preparation time 10 minutes
Cooking time 8 minutes
To serve 6

You will need

2 oz. uncooked chicken breast
1 teaspoon cornflour
2 teaspoons cold water
2 oz. mushrooms
2 oz. bamboo shoots
3½ pints (U.S. 9 cups) hot chicken stock
2 teaspoons soya sauce
½ teaspoon salt
3 spring onions, chopped

Shred chicken; blend cornflour with water and add to chicken. Slice mushrooms and bamboo shoots; simmer for 5 minutes in the hot stock. Add chicken and continue to simmer until meat turns white. Stir in soya sauce and salt. Garnish with spring onions.

KAI YUNG SUK MAI TONG
MINCED CHICKEN AND CORN CHOWDER WITH ALMONDS

Preparation time 10 minutes
Cooking time 8–10 minutes
To serve 4–6

You will need

11-oz. can creamed sweet corn
1 teaspoon cornflour
2 tablespoons cold water
2 teaspoons salt
½ teaspoon pepper
3½ pints (U.S. 9 cups) hot chicken stock
12 oz. uncooked breast of chicken, minced
2 egg whites, beaten
2 tablespoons roasted almonds, chopped

Put the sweet corn through a mincer or liquidiser, to break up any kernels.
Blend the cornflour with the water; add to the corn. Season with salt and pepper and stir into the hot stock.
Pound the chicken until smooth and add the egg

whites. Add to corn soup. Bring to the boil, then simmer very gently for 8–10 minutes. Sprinkle with almonds and serve.

DUMPLINGS

HAR GOW
STEAMED PRAWN DUMPLINGS

Preparation time 20 minutes
Cooking time 13 minutes
To serve 6–8

You will need

1 tablespoon lard
4 oz. pork, minced
2 mushrooms, finely chopped
2 spring onions, finely chopped
4 Pacific prawns, peeled and chopped
2 tablespoons bamboo shoots, diced
1 thin slice ginger, finely chopped
½ teaspoon sesame oil
pinch salt
pinch monosodium glutamate (optional)
2 teaspoons light soya sauce
¼ teaspoon sugar
1 tablespoon Chinese wine *or* sherry
½ teaspoon cornflour
2 tablespoons cold water
6 oz. Chinese wheat starch *or* flour
generous ¼ pint (U.S. ¾ cup) boiling water

Heat lard in frying pan and toss the pork in it for 30 seconds. Add mushrooms, spring onions, prawns, bamboo shoots, ginger and sesame oil. Scramble for 30 seconds, season with salt, monosodium glutamate, soya sauce and sugar. Sprinkle in the wine.
Blend the cornflour with the cold water, pour it over the contents of the frying pan, stir well and turn mixture out into a bowl. In a separate bowl, mix wheat starch or flour with boiling water to a stiff dough, adding the water very gradually. Knead well, sprinkle with dry flour and roll into a long sausage. Pinch off small pieces of dough about the size of a walnut, roll out into circles 3 inches in diameter, press down with end of rolling pin, and pull edges to make extra thin, and slightly fluted. Put a good teaspoon of the filling in the middle of each circle of dough, pinch the edges together to form a semi-circle, steam for 12 minutes and serve piping hot.

SHAO MAI
PORK AND PRAWN STEAMED DUMPLINGS

Preparation time 20 minutes
Cooking time 15 minutes
To serve 6–8

You will need

Chinese noodle paste (see page 82) using half the quantity
8 oz. pork, minced (lean and fat)
4 oz. cooked, peeled prawns
1 tablespoon chopped water chestnuts
1 tablespoon chopped bamboo shoots
pinch salt
pinch sugar
pinch monosodium glutamate (optional)
1 teaspoon light soya sauce
pinch grated ginger
1 tablespoon Chinese wine *or* sherry

Prepare the dough, knead well, wrap in a damp cloth and leave until the filling is ready. Put pork in a mixing bowl. Reserve 6–8 prawns for decoration and chop the rest. Combine pork and chopped prawns with the rest of the ingredients, blend well. Break off uniform pieces of dough, roll each piece into a thin circle and flatten and flute the edges by scraping with the edge of a saucer. Put 3 teaspoons filling in the centre of each piece of pastry and pinch the edges to close around the filling, but leave the top free.
Garnish the top of each shao mai with a whole prawn, and steam them for 15 minutes. Serve at once.

Anke's roast pork dumplings (see recipe page 86)

CHAR SHIU BAO
ANKE'S ROAST PORK DUMPLINGS
(Illustrated in black and white on page 85)

Preparation time 22 minutes
Cooking time 23 minutes
To serve 6

You will need

6 oz. lean roast pork, finely chopped
4 tablespoons peanut oil
1 teaspoon soya sauce
pinch salt
pinch monosodium glutamate (optional)
1 tablespoon sugar
1 teaspoon cornflour
2 teaspoons oyster sauce
6 oz. plain flour
½ teaspoon baking powder

Fry the pork in 1 tablespoon oil, stirring all the time, for 45–50 seconds. Sprinkle with soya sauce, salt, monosodium glutamate and 1 teaspoon sugar. Blend half the cornflour with 3 tablespoons cold water and stir it into the pork. Cook for 1½ minutes, constantly stirring the mixture, which should be quite dry. Remove from heat.
Mix remaining cornflour with oyster sauce and blend into the pork, and leave to cool.
While the pork stuffing is cooling, prepare the dough. Sift the plain flour on to a pastry board, make a well in the centre, sprinkle in baking powder and remaining sugar. Add remaining oil and 2 tablespoons cold water. Mix well and knead into a stiff dough. Cut the dough and roll into fat sausage shapes between the palms of your hands. Break off uniform pieces, roll to the size of a ping-pong ball and flatten each into a circle about 2½ inches in diameter.
Put a portion of roast pork filling in the centre of each circle of dough and pinch up the edges with fingers, turning to shape the dumplings. Alternatively, put the flattened circle of dough on a lightly floured cloth, fill with stuffing, then hold the cloth with the circle of dough in the left hand and twist the end of the cloth tightly, to mould the dough into a round bun with a twisted top.
Place each dumpling on a small square of waxed paper and place in a steamer, about 1 inch apart. Steam over rapidly boiling water for 20 minutes. Serve piping hot with pickles, if liked.

FISH AND SHELLFISH

TONG CHO LOONG HAR
SWEET AND SOUR LOBSTER WITH PINEAPPLE
(Illustrated in black and white on page 92)

Preparation time 5 minutes plus 20 minutes standing time
Cooking time 8 minutes
To serve 4

You will need

1 lb. lobster meat
salt
2 tablespoons sugar
2 teaspoons soya sauce
oil for deep frying
2–3 tablespoons plain flour
2 eggs, lightly beaten
8-oz. can pineapple cubes, drained
2 teaspoons peanut oil
water
2 tablespoons vinegar
2 teaspoons cornflour

Cut the lobster into bite-sized pieces. Sprinkle with 1 teaspoon salt, 1 teaspoon sugar and the soya sauce and leave to macerate for 20 minutes.
Heat the oil and while it is heating, roll the lobster pieces lightly in flour, then dip into beaten egg and drop them one by one into the hot oil. Deep-fry until golden and drain on greaseproof paper.
While the lobster pieces are cooking, cut pineapple cubes in half and prepare the sauce.
Mix together in a pan the peanut oil, 2 tablespoons water, vinegar, the rest of the sugar and 1 teaspoon salt. Bring to the boil, add pineapple pieces, and cornflour blended with enough water to make a thin paste. Remove from heat, put in the lobster pieces; make sure they are well immersed in the sauce, and serve immediately, with boiled rice and Prawn Crackers (see page 83).

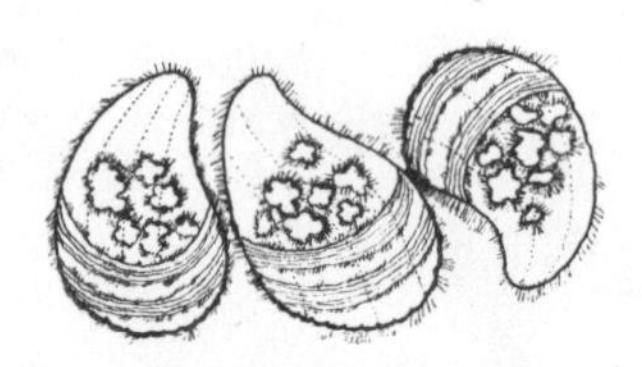

Sweet and sour pork (see recipe page 105)

Above: Winter melon soup (see recipe page 83)

Above right: Fried bream with black beans (see recipe page 92)

Right: Silver and gold soup (see recipe page 84)

Top: Bream with black beans
Bottom: Silver and gold soup

Left to right: Chicken with peaches and almonds (see recipe page 98), ginger pears with lychees (see recipe page 106). In background preserved ginger and boiled rice with peas and prawns

GUNG PIN LOONG HAR
GINGER LOBSTER

Preparation time 11 minutes
Cooking time 10 minutes
To serve 2

You will need

1 tablespoon cornflour
2 tablespoons oil
4 oz. mushrooms, sliced
1 large lettuce heart, shredded
8 oz. lobster meat, diced
1 teaspoon finely chopped fresh ginger
4 or 5 spring onions, chopped

Mix cornflour with a little water to make a thin paste. Heat half the oil and fry mushrooms and lettuce for 3 minutes. Remove. Add rest of oil. Dip lobster into cornflour paste and fry for 3 minutes. Then add the fried vegetables and cook together for 3 minutes. Add ginger and spring onions, stir well, and serve.

LOONG HAR FU YONG
LOBSTER OMELETTE

Preparation time 3 minutes
Cooking time 5 minutes
To serve 6

You will need

8 oz. lobster meat
1 tablespoon oil
1 tablespoon chopped onion
salt
6 eggs, beaten
pinch freshly ground pepper

Dice the lobster meat. Heat oil, add the onion and cook gently for 30 seconds. Add lobster, cook for 2 minutes, season with salt to taste. Pour on eggs, mix quickly, cook for 1 minute, sprinkle with pepper, shake the pan carefully to ensure even cooking. Cook for a further minute and serve at once.

GUNG PIN LOO YU
BASS WITH GINGER SAUCE

Preparation time 3 minutes
Cooking time 11 minutes
To serve 4–6

You will need

1½–2 lb. bass, cleaned
1 teaspoon oil
2 teaspoons soya sauce
2 teaspoons fresh ginger, finely chopped *or*
 1 teaspoon ground ginger
4 spring onions, chopped

Bring a large pan of salted water to the boil, and put in the fish. As soon as boiling is re-established, reduce heat and simmer for 6 minutes. Drain fish carefully and arrange on a serving dish. Combine together oil, soya sauce and ginger, and pour over the fish. Garnish with spring onions and serve with plain boiled rice (see page 80).

DIM SIN YU YIN
FISH BALLS WITH SWEET AND SOUR SAUCE

Preparation time 5 minutes
Cooking time 4 minutes
To serve 4

You will need

1½ lb. boned fish, flaked
salt and pepper
1 egg
4 oz. cornflour
oil for deep frying
sweet and sour sauce (see page 103)
4 or 5 spring onions, chopped

Season the flaked fish with salt and pepper, add egg and cornflour. Stir until the mixture is smooth, shape into small balls. Fry them in oil until golden. Drain, then cover with sweet and sour sauce, garnish with chopped spring onions. Serve plain boiled rice (see page 80) separately.

LOONG HAR CHOW MAI
FRIED LOBSTER WITH RICE NOODLES

Preparation time 12 minutes plus 30 minutes standing time
Cooking time 6 minutes
To serve 2

You will need

6 oz. thick rice noodles
1 tablespoon oil
8 oz. lobster meat, diced
3 oz. bean sprouts
4 medium mushrooms, sliced
2 oz. cucumber, sliced
2 oz. water chestnuts, sliced
2 oz. bamboo shoots, sliced
1 stick celery, sliced
4 tablespoons sliced onion
½ teaspoon salt
1 teaspoon sugar
2 teaspoons soya sauce
stock

Put the noodles in a bowl, cover with hot water and leave to stand for 30 minutes. Heat the oil in a pan and sauté the lobster for 1 minute. Add all the vegetables and cook together for 1 minute. Add salt, sugar, soya sauce and enough stock to cover. Cook for 1 minute, add drained noodles, cook for 2 minutes and serve.

DOW SEE YU
FRIED BREAM WITH BLACK BEANS

(Illustrated in colour on page 89)

Preparation time 3 minutes
Cooking time 11 minutes
To serve 4

You will need

one bream (1–1½ lb.) cleaned
salt
flour
1 oz. black soya beans
1 clove garlic, crushed
1 teaspoon soya sauce
1 teaspoon brandy
4 tablespoons oil
2 teaspoons cornflour
½ pint (U.S. 1¼ cups) water

Make a few shallow incisions, slantways, on both sides of the fish. Sprinkle with salt and coat with flour, making sure it adheres properly.
Scald the soya beans and mix with garlic, soya sauce and brandy. Heat the oil in a large pan and fry the fish until golden. Put on a large serving dish and keep hot. Pour surplus oil from the pan and fry the black bean mixture for 2 minutes, stirring constantly. Blend cornflour with water, add to the pan and cook for 2 minutes, stirring all the time. Pour over the fish and serve with plain boiled rice (see page 80).

Sweet and sour lobster with pineapple (see recipe page 86)

HUNG YEN HAR
PRAWNS STUFFED WITH ALMONDS

This is the first Chinese dish I ever saw cooked and it floats up to me from my remote childhood – still a lovely dream.

Preparation time 22 minutes
Cooking time 7–8 minutes
To serve 4

You will need

1 lb. large, uncooked prawns
2 rashers lean bacon
2 oz. blanched, roasted almonds
salt
1 egg, beaten
flour
oil for deep frying

Peel the prawns, leaving the tail tips on. Make 2 slits in each prawn without opening them out. Shred bacon and almonds, and mix together. Put ½ teaspoon of this mixture into each slit in the prawn and press the edges of the slits gently together to seal. Season with salt to taste. Dip into the egg, dredge lightly with flour and deep-fry in hot oil until golden. Drain on absorbent paper and serve at once.

KAI JOP MUN YEE
BREAM WITH TOMATOES

Preparation time 3 minutes
Cooking time 10 minutes
To serve 4

You will need

1–1½ lb. whole bream, cleaned
salt
flour
4 tablespoons oil
8 oz. ripe tomatoes, skinned
1 clove garlic, crushed
1 teaspoon sugar
1 teaspoon sherry
1 teaspoon cornflour
¼ pint (U.S. ⅔ cup) water
1 spring onion

Make a few light incisions, slantways, on both sides of fish, taking care not to cut too deeply. Sprinkle with salt and dredge with flour. Heat oil in pan and cook fish gently until brown. Remove and keep hot. Pour excess oil from the pan, add tomatoes cut into quarters, and garlic. Cook 1 minute.
Blend sugar, sherry and cornflour with the water and add to the pan. Simmer for 2 minutes. Cut the spring onion into 2-inch strips, then, with a sharp knife, slice strips lengthways. Pour the sauce over the fish, sprinkle with spring onion strips and serve with boiled rice (see page 80).

CHOW YU PIN
FRIED PLAICE

Preparation time 13 minutes
Cooking time 8 minutes
To serve 2

You will need

oil for frying
2 oz. onion, chopped
1 stick celery, diced
2 oz. water chestnuts, sliced
3 oz. bamboo shoots, sliced
2 oz. cucumber, sliced
4 medium mushrooms, sliced
stock
8 oz. plaice fillets
½ teaspoon pepper
1 tablespoon Chinese wine *or* sherry
1 teaspoon cornflour
1 teaspoon soya sauce
few drops sesame oil

Heat a little oil in a pan and quick-fry the vegetables, allowing no more than 1 minute. Add enough stock to cover and simmer, covered, for 1 minute. Cut the fish into thin slices, and place in another hot, oiled pan, adding pepper and wine. Cook for 1 minute, turning carefully. Add vegetables to the fish and cook for a further 2 minutes. Blend the cornflour with 2 tablespoons cold water, add to pan, stirring gently. Season with soya sauce, sprinkle with sesame oil, cook for 1 minute and serve.

Prawns with peppers and pineapple

GONG BOR LOW HAR KOW
PRAWNS WITH PEPPERS AND PINEAPPLE

(Illustrated in black and white above)

Preparation time 5 minutes
Cooking time 9 minutes
To serve 4

You will need

1 lb. shelled prawns, fresh or frozen
1 lb. green sweet peppers
2 tablespoons oil
salt
1 knob green ginger, shredded
1 teaspoon sugar
2 teaspoons soya sauce
4 tablespoons pineapple pieces
1 teaspoon sherry
1 teaspoon cornflour

Pick over prawns. If frozen allow to thaw. Wash green peppers, discard core and seeds, and slice into half rings. Heat 1 tablespoon of the oil in a pan, add ½ teaspoon salt and quickly toss peppers for 7 to 8 seconds. Add 1 tablespoon water, simmer for 3 minutes, remove from pan and keep hot. Heat the rest of the oil, add ½ teaspoon salt and the ginger and sauté the prawns quickly for 30 seconds. Add sugar, soya sauce, pineapple, sherry and 2 tablespoons water. Simmer for 3 minutes, add peppers and their juice, mix, and cook together for 1 minute. Stir in the cornflour, blended with just enough water to make a thin paste. Cook 1 minute. Serve with plain boiled rice or noodles.

HAI YUK
STEWED CRAB

Preparation time 7 minutes
Cooking time 10 minutes
To serve 4

You will need

2 large, soft-shell crabs
4 tablespoons oil
1 clove garlic, crushed
1 teaspoon salt
4 oz. pork, freshly minced
2 tablespoons soya sauce
1 teaspoon sugar
½ teaspoon pepper
½ pint (U.S. 1¼ cups) boiling clear stock
1 teaspoon cornflour
3 tablespoons cold water
1 egg, lightly beaten
2–3 spring onions, chopped

Cut each crab into 6–8 pieces. Heat oil with the garlic, add salt and pork and brown lightly. Stir in the soya sauce, add the sugar, pepper and boiling stock. Add the crabs, mix well, cover and simmer for 7–8 minutes. Mix the cornflour with the cold water, stir into the pan until the sauce is smooth. Remove from the heat, stir in the egg, sprinkle with spring onions and serve at once.

TO FOU HAR YEN
BEAN CURD WITH PRAWNS
(Illustrated in colour on page 77)

Preparation time 2 minutes
Cooking time 3 minutes
To serve 4

You will need

8 oz. bean curd
3–4 tablespoons peanut oil
4 oz. peeled prawns
4 oz. frozen peas
1 tablespoon sherry
2 teaspoons soya sauce
½ teaspoon salt
½ teaspoon pepper

Cut the bean curd into oblong pieces, put them in a frying basket. Dip into boiling water for 10 seconds. Drain.
Heat oil to boiling point, throw in the prawns, cook for 10 seconds. Add bean curd and cook together for 1 minute. Add peas and cook for a further minute. Add sherry, soya sauce, salt and pepper. Turn off heat. Stir gently and serve.

YING DAN
STEAMED EGGS WITH PRAWNS OR MUSHROOMS

Preparation time 6 minutes
Cooking time 15 minutes
To serve 4

You will need

4–6 eggs
3 tablespoons water
2 teaspoons soya sauce
½ teaspoon salt
3–4 spring onions, chopped
4 oz. peeled prawns *or* 2 oz. fresh mushrooms, sliced

Beat the eggs with the water. Add the rest of the ingredients and mix well. Pour into a large heat-proof dish, or into individual ramekins, and steam for 15 minutes.

YEUNG MOW GOO
MUSHROOMS STUFFED WITH SHRIMPS

Preparation time 6 minutes
Cooking time 12 minutes
To serve 4

You will need

8 large mushrooms
4 oz. peeled shrimps
1 tablespoon butter
4 tablespoons minced pork
1 tablespoon finely chopped celery
¼ teaspoon ground ginger
salt and pepper
2 tablespoons oil
1 teaspoon soya sauce

Remove stems from the mushrooms and wipe the caps. Chop shrimps and stems; toss in hot butter to warm through. Mix shrimps with pork, celery and ginger, and season with salt and pepper to taste. Fill mushrooms (gill side) with mixture.
Heat oil in a pan, put in mushrooms, stuffed side up, sprinkle with soya sauce, cover and simmer for 10 minutes.

HAR KOW KAN CHOY
PRAWNS WITH CELERY

Preparation time 5 minutes
Cooking time 9 minutes
To serve 4

You will need

1 tablespoon olive oil
8 oz. cooked, peeled prawns
1 small onion, sliced
2 oz. mushrooms, chopped
3 sticks celery, sliced
pinch pepper
1 teaspoon soya sauce
1 teaspoon brandy
1 teaspoon cornflour
¼ pint (U.S. ⅔ cup) water
4–5 spring onions, cut in 2–inch strips

Heat the oil in a pan and fry prawns and onion together for 3 minutes, stirring constantly. Add mushrooms, celery and pepper. Cook for 4 minutes. Mix soya sauce, brandy, cornflour and water, stir into the pan and cook for 1 minute. Remove from heat, sprinkle with spring onions and serve.

HAR LUK
DEEP-FRIED PRAWNS

Preparation time 12 minutes
Cooking time 7–8 minutes
To serve 4

You will need

1 lb. large prawns
1 teaspoon sugar
1 oz. flour
½ teaspoon salt
¼ teaspoon pepper
1 egg, lightly beaten
oil for deep frying

Wash and shell prawns, leaving tail tips on. Remove dark veins, wash and drain.
Slit the middle, turn the tail up and pull through the slit.
Sift the sugar, flour, salt and pepper together, and mix with the egg.
Dip the prawns into this mixture, place in a frying basket and deep-fry until golden. Serve with green salad.

PRAWN SAMPANS

Preparation time 12 minutes
Cooking time 30 seconds
To serve 8

You will need

8 oz. peeled prawns
3 egg whites
2 spring onions, chopped
1 teaspoon ground ginger
1 teaspoon soya sauce
salt and pepper
8 slices French bread
oil for deep frying

Chop the prawns coarsely. Mix egg whites, onions, ginger, and soya sauce. Add prawns.

Season to taste with salt and pepper and whisk vigorously. Cut crusts off the bread slices and trim into boat shapes to make 16 'sampans'. Spread generously with prawn mixture, piling it up and patting down well.
Heat the oil. Put 'sampans' into frying basket and lower into oil for 10 seconds, which is ample time to deep-fry them pale golden. Drain well and serve at once.

DAN CHIN HAR
PACIFIC PRAWNS WITH LETTUCE

Preparation time 18 minutes
Cooking time 5 minutes
To serve 4

You will need

1 lb. large prawns
salt
2–3 slices ginger, pounded
2 teaspoons cornflour
1 crisp lettuce, washed
1 tablespoon oil
1 clove garlic, crushed
freshly ground pepper
$\frac{1}{4}$ pint (U.S. $\frac{2}{3}$ cup) water

Peel prawns (Dublin Bay or the large Pacific kind are best for this dish), leaving tail tips on. Then split lengthways and remove dark veins. Place prawns on a plate, sprinkle with a pinch of salt, the ginger and cornflour. Shred the lettuce coarsely.
Heat oil in a pan with garlic, add prawns and sauté briskly. As soon as the prawns change colour, add the lettuce. Cook for 1 minute, season with pepper, add more salt if necessary. Pour in the water, bring to the boil, stir and serve.

POULTRY AND GAME

KAI SEE CHOW KAN CHOY TUNG GOO
CHICKEN WITH CELERY AND MUSHROOMS
(Illustrated in black and white below)

Preparation time 10 minutes
Cooking time 11 minutes
To serve 4–6

You will need

1 lb. uncooked chicken meat
1 head celery
2 tablespoons lard
2 oz. mushrooms, sliced
1 tablespoon soya sauce
1 tablespoon cornflour
4 tablespoons stock *or* cold water

Cut chicken meat into thin slices. String and cut the celery into bite-sized pieces. Fry the chicken in lard for 5 minutes, stirring all the time. Add celery and mushrooms, stir well and season with soya sauce. Cook, stirring frequently, for 3 minutes.
Blend cornflour with stock, stir into the pan. Simmer for 2 minutes and serve.

Chicken with celery and mushrooms

NGAP SZECHWAN
FRAGRANT CRISP DUCK, SZECHWAN STYLE

Preparation time 20 minutes
Cooking time 1 hour 55 minutes – 2 hours 10 minutes
To serve 6

You will need

peanut *or* other vegetable oil for deep frying
4-lb. duck
soya sauce
2 tablespoons spring onions, chopped
¼ pint (U.S. ⅔ cup) chicken stock *or* water
12 oz. peeled shrimps *or* prawns, chopped
4 oz. fat pork, diced
2 eggs
monosodium glutamate (optional)
salt
cornflour

Heat the oil. Open the duck by cutting along the back. Brush with soya sauce. Using a frying basket, deep-fry duck in the oil until brown; drain. (This operation helps to seal the skin.) Take a pan just large enough to hold the duck and line it with spring onions. Lay the duck on top, add stock, cover and simmer gently for 1 hour 30 minutes–1 hour 45 minutes until tender. Remove and carefully bone the duck through the opening along the back without breaking the skin. Remove the meat, keeping the skin whole.
Dice the duck meat and mix with shrimps and pork. Bind with one egg, season to taste with monosodium glutamate and salt, mix well and put the mixture into the duck skin. Carefully stitch up the opening. Beat remaining egg. Heat the oil again. Roll the duck in cornflour, coat with beaten egg, lower into the hot oil in a frying basket and deep-fry until pale gold. Drain; arrange on a heated serving platter. Reboil and strain the stock and serve separately.

Note
This is a Szechwan speciality and well worth the trouble of making.

HUNG YEN KAI
CHICKEN WITH PEACHES AND ALMONDS

(Illustrated in colour on page 90 and black and white below)

Preparation time 27 minutes plus 20 minutes standing time
Cooking time 34–36 minutes
To serve 6

You will need

2 tablespoons soya sauce
1 tablespoon oil
1 tablespoon sherry
2 teaspoons lemon juice
1 teaspoon monosodium glutamate (optional)
3-lb. chicken
butter
1 tablespoon oil
2 small onions, cut in chunks
1 green sweet pepper, deseeded and chopped
4 oz. button mushrooms, quartered
8-oz. can sliced peaches
1 tablespoon cornflour
salt and pepper
1½ oz. blanched almonds
watercress

Chicken with peaches and almonds

Mix together the first 5 ingredients and pour into a bowl or deep plate. This is the marinade. Skin and joint the chicken. Cut the meat from the bones.
Simmer chicken bones in 1 pint (U.S. 2½ cups) water for stock. Meanwhile, cut chicken meat into bite-sized pieces and soak in the marinade for about 20 minutes, turning occasionally.
Drain chicken pieces, keeping the marinade for the sauce. Heat 1 oz. butter and oil in a heavy pan. Add chicken and cook gently for 3–4 minutes until sealed on all sides. Remove chicken. Put in the onion pieces and cook for one minute. Add the green pepper and cook for another minute. Add the quartered mushrooms and cook again for a minute, then add chicken. Drain the juice from the peaches and blend it smoothly with the cornflour. Stir in the remains of the marinade, ¼ pint (U.S. ⅔ cup) chicken stock and seasoning to taste. Pour over the chicken, stir till boiling. Cover and simmer 3–4 minutes. Add the peaches, and cook for another minute. Fry the blanched almonds in a little butter until golden. Put the chicken on a serving plate and garnish with almonds and watercress. Serve with boiled rice (see page 80), garnished with cooked peas and cooked shrimps, Prawn Crackers (see page 83) and China tea.

HOP TO KAI DING
CHICKEN WITH WALNUTS

Preparation time 12 minutes
Cooking time 10 minutes
To serve 4

You will need

4 oz. fresh mushrooms
8 oz. uncooked chicken, diced
2 teaspoons soya sauce
2 teaspoons brandy
1 teaspoon cornflour
salt
1 tablespoon oil
1 clove garlic, crushed
2 teaspoons oyster sauce
2 sticks celery, diced
4 oz. walnuts, shelled and skinned
¼ pint (U.S. ⅔ cup) water
2 spring onions, chopped (optional)

Cut mushrooms into ¼-inch slices. Combine chicken with soya sauce, brandy, cornflour and salt to taste. Heat oil in a pan and brown garlic in it. Remove garlic and sauté chicken briskly for 2 minutes without allowing it to brown. Add oyster sauce, mushrooms and celery. Simmer for 5 minutes, stirring constantly. Add walnuts and water. Simmer for 2 minutes and serve.
Garnish with chopped spring onions, if liked.

KAI SEE CHOW SUB GUM
FRIED CHICKEN WITH MIXED VEGETABLES

Preparation time 8 minutes
Cooking time 5 minutes
To serve 4

You will need

oil
1 small onion, chopped
2 oz. water chestnuts, sliced
2 oz. mushrooms, sliced
2 sticks celery, sliced
2 oz. cucumber, sliced
salt
sugar
soya sauce
chicken stock
4 oz. fried chicken, sliced
1 teaspoon cornflour
2 tablespoons cold water
½ teaspoon sesame oil
1 teaspoon roasted almonds, ground

Heat a pan with sufficient oil to grease base and sides. Put in all the vegetables and cook, stirring, for 1 minute. Add salt and sugar to taste, a little soya sauce and enough stock to cover. Simmer, covered, for 1 minute.
Add chicken, cornflour blended with the water, and sesame oil. Cook for 2 minutes. Transfer to a serving dish, sprinkle with almonds and serve.

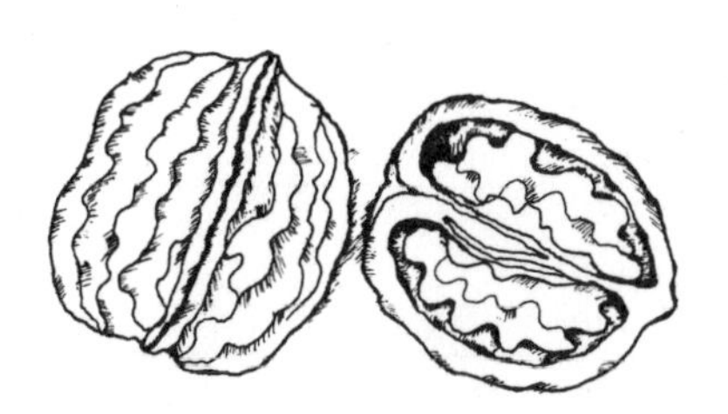

DIM SIN KAI
SWEET AND SOUR CHICKEN

Preparation time 7 minutes
Cooking time 5 minutes
To serve 4

You will need

¼ chicken, boned
salt
cornflour
1 egg, beaten
1 tablespoon oil
sweet and sour sauce (see page 103)

Shred the chicken, sprinkle with salt. Spread cornflour on a sheet of greaseproof paper. Dip chicken in the egg and then in the cornflour. Heat oil in a pan and fry the chicken briskly for 2 minutes, stirring constantly.
Add sweet and sour sauce, stir, simmer for 3 minutes and serve.

HOI YOW KAI KOW
CHICKEN STRIPS IN OYSTER SAUCE

Preparation time 16 minutes
Cooking time 22 minutes
To serve 6

You will need

1 lb. boned uncooked chicken
2 teaspoons cornflour
½ teaspoon sugar
1 teaspoon soya sauce
pinch salt
3 oz. bamboo shoots
1 oz. chives
¼ oz. fresh ginger
6 spring onions
1 tablespoon peanut oil
1 tablespoon oyster sauce
2 tablespoons water

Cut chicken meat into thin strips. Put in a bowl, sprinkle with 1 teaspoon cornflour, the sugar, soya sauce and salt. Mix well and leave to stand. Bring bamboo shoots to the boil in enough salted water to cover, lower heat and simmer for 15 minutes. Drain and cut into strips the same size as chicken. Cut chives into 1-inch lengths. Chop ginger and onions together very finely. Toss bamboo shoots in a hot frying pan without any grease, to dry them off. Shake the pan and stir to prevent burning.
Heat the oil in a pan, and fry ginger and onion for 2 minutes. Add chicken and fry, stirring all the time, for 2 minutes. Add the bamboo shoots, stir carefully, cook for 1 minute. Stir in the chives and oyster sauce. Blend remaining cornflour with water, stir into the pan, and cook for 1 minute to thicken the sauce.

HAR PENG KAI
CHICKEN IN WHITE CLOUD

Preparation time 13 minutes plus 15 minutes standing time
Cooking time 45–50 minutes
Oven temperature 191°C., 375°F., Gas Mark 5
To serve 6–8

You will need

3-lb. chicken
salt
3 cloves garlic
3–4 leeks
2 tablespoons sherry
1 tablespoon dark soya sauce
1 tablespoon honey
prawn crackers (see page 83)

Rub the chicken with salt. Crush the garlic, cut the leeks into 2-inch chunks. Sprinkle with 1 teaspoon each of the sherry and soya sauce and use for stuffing the chicken. Stitch up the opening. Turn on oven at temperature given above. Mix the remaining sherry, soya sauce and honey, rub into the chicken and leave for 15 minutes. Brush the chicken with the sherry mixture again and put into preheated oven. Turn from time to time brushing with the sherry mixture so that the bird is nicely brown all over.
Cook for 45–50 minutes.
Remove the chicken from the oven, cut up, and arrange on a heated serving dish in as near its original shape as you can. Cover with freshly made prawn crackers (to make the 'white cloud') and serve.

Deep-fried chicken legs

CHAR JEE KAI
DEEP-FRIED CHICKEN LEGS
(Illustrated in black and white above)

Preparation time 2 minutes
Cooking time 9 minutes
To serve 4–8

You will need

fat for deep frying
8 chicken legs
salt and pepper
8 cutlet frills

GARNISH
sliced vegetables in season

Heat fat and deep-fry chicken legs for about 7 minutes or until tender. Drain chicken on absorbent paper. Mix salt and pepper in equal proportions, and sprinkle on to chicken. Place a cutlet frill on the thin end of each leg to hide the bone, and arrange on a serving dish, thick ends towards the centre. Garnish centre of dish with slices of vegetable of choice in season. Serve with a selection of sauces, pickles and salted peanuts.

TUNG GOO MAN KAI
CHICKEN AND MUSHROOMS

Preparation time 15 minutes
Cooking time 8–9 minutes
To serve 4

You will need

half a $3\frac{1}{2}$-lb. chicken
salt
2 teaspoons soya sauce
2 teaspoons brandy
2 teaspoons cornflour
1 knob green ginger, chopped
1 tablespoon oil
8 oz. fresh mushrooms
2 cloves garlic, crushed
2 teaspoons oyster sauce
$\frac{1}{2}$ pint (U.S. $1\frac{1}{4}$ cups) water
3–4 spring onions, chopped

Bone the chicken, dice it and sprinkle with salt to taste. Mix chicken with soya sauce, brandy, cornflour, ginger and $\frac{1}{2}$ teaspoon oil. Blend well. Slice the mushrooms. Heat the remaining oil in a pan with the garlic, allow garlic to brown, add the chicken, stirring constantly until half cooked (2–3 minutes). Add the oyster sauce and mushrooms, stir, and cook for 3 minutes. Add the water and mix well. Cook for 1 minute. Sprinkle with spring onions and serve.

JEE BOW KAI
PAPER-WRAPPED DEEP-FRIED CHICKEN

(Illustrated in black and white below)

Preparation time 17 minutes
Cooking time 4–5 minutes
To serve 4

You will need

8 oz. uncooked chicken meat
1 tablespoon ginger-flavoured sherry (see page 106)
1 small clove garlic, finely chopped
1 small onion, finely chopped
¼ teaspoon sesame oil
1–2 slices ginger, finely chopped
pinch salt
pinch monosodium glutamate (optional)
2 tablespoons finely chopped bamboo shoots
1 teaspoon soya sauce
eight 6-inch squares of greaseproof paper
peanut oil for deep frying

Cut the chicken into neat small cubes. Put in a bowl, add the rest of the ingredients up to and including the soya sauce, mix well with the fingertips. Leave, to allow all the ingredients to mix their flavours. Rub each square of greaseproof paper with a little peanut oil. Divide the chicken into 8 portions. Put a portion of chicken mixture on one corner of the paper. Fold the corner over, then fold in sides and tuck in the flap. When all the packages are made, heat the oil. To test the temperature, drop in a piece of potato. If the temperature is right, it should rise rather than pop up.
Deep-fry the chicken parcels for 4–5 minutes, to brown nicely.
This delectable dish should be served at once. If you attempt to keep it warm in the oven, the chicken will get tough. Neither is reheating successful.
The guests help themselves to the packets, unwrap their own chicken parcels and eat them straight from the paper with all the juices retained.

DOW SEE NGAP
DUCK WITH BLACK BEANS

Preparation time 10 minutes plus 5 minutes standing time
Cooking time 5 minutes
To serve 4

You will need

8 oz. roast duck, sliced
½ teaspoon salt
pinch sugar
pinch monosodium glutamate (optional)
few drops sesame oil
1 teaspoon soya sauce
2 tablespoons cornflour
4 slices fresh ginger
2 tablespoons canned black beans
1 clove garlic, crushed
1 tablespoon chopped onion
2 tablespoons peanut oil
¼ pint (U.S. ⅔ cup) chicken stock (or water with a stock cube)
1 tablespoon Chinese wine *or* sherry
2 tablespoons cold water

Put duck meat in a bowl, sprinkle with salt, sugar, monosodium glutamate, sesame oil, soya sauce and 1 tablespoon cornflour. Mix well and leave to marinate for 5 minutes.
Chop the ginger with the beans, add the garlic and pound together to a paste. Fry the onion in peanut oil for 1 minute, without allowing it to brown. Add black bean paste and cook, stirring all the time, for 1 minute. Add duck, stir and moisten with stock and wine. Cook for 1 minute. Check seasoning, adding more salt or monosodium glutamate, if necessary. Blend the remaining cornflour with the cold water, stir into the pan, and cook for 1 minute until the sauce thickens. Serve.

Paper-wrapped deep-fried chicken

DIM SIN
SWEET AND SOUR SAUCE

Preparation time 2–10 minutes
Cooking time 3 minutes
To serve 4

You will need

1 tablespoon peanut oil
4 tablespoons water
2 tablespoons vinegar
2 teaspoons sugar
pinch salt
8 oz. fresh pineapple, shredded or 8-oz. can shredded pineapple, drained
1 tablespoon cornflour

Heat the peanut oil. Add 2 tablespoons water, the vinegar, sugar and salt. Bring to the boil, add pineapple. Blend the cornflour with remaining 2 tablespoons cold water and mix into the sauce. Stir over low heat until the sauce thickens slightly – this is a matter of seconds. Remove from heat and use as required.

LEMON-FLAVOURED CHICKEN

Preparation time 9 minutes
Cooking time 1 hour
Oven temperature 218°C., 425°F., Gas Mark 7
To serve 6

You will need

4-lb. chicken
1 tablespoon soya sauce
1 lemon, cut in thin slices
1 tablespoon Chinese wine *or* sherry
1 tablespoon sugar
1 teaspoon monosodium glutamate (optional)
½ pint (U.S. 1¼ cups) chicken stock (or water with a stock cube)

Turn on oven at temperature given above. Put chicken in an ovenproof dish. Brush with soya sauce. Sprinkle lemon slices with wine, sugar and monosodium glutamate, mix well and cover the chicken with them all. Add stock, cover and cook in preheated oven for about 1 hour. Remove chicken, chop into pieces and arrange on a heated serving dish with the pan juices poured over.

KAI SEE JAR MIN
CHICKEN CHOW MEIN

(Illustrated in black and white below)

Preparation time 9 minutes
Cooking time 13–14 minutes
To serve 6

You will need

6 oz. uncooked chicken, sliced
6 oz. uncooked lean pork, sliced
salt
½ teaspoon monosodium glutamate (optional)
1 teaspoon soya sauce
1 teaspoon brandy (optional)
1 tablespoon cornflour
oil
1½ lb. noodles, cooked
1 clove garlic, crushed
2 teaspoons oyster sauce
pepper
1 onion, sliced
3 sticks celery, diced
2 tablespoons cold water
2 tablespoons cooked peas

Place chicken and pork in a bowl, add a little salt, monosodium glutamate, soya sauce, brandy, half the cornflour and 1 teaspoon oil. Mix well. Heat enough oil to cover bottom of a pan, and fry noodles quickly for 1–2 minutes. (They should be crisp on the outside and soft inside.) Remove, drain and keep hot.

Heat 1 tablespoon oil with the garlic and fry chicken and pork mixture for 5 minutes. Add oyster sauce, salt and pepper to taste, onion and celery, and cook for 5 minutes. Blend remainder of the cornflour with the cold water, add to the pan and bring to the boil. Stir; add the peas. Pour the mixture over the noodles and serve.

Chicken chow mein

BOR LOW NGAP
FRIED DUCK WITH PINEAPPLE
(Illustrated in colour on front cover)

Preparation time 7 minutes
Cooking time 6 minutes
To serve 4

You will need

8 oz. boned uncooked duck
1 large fresh pineapple (or 1-lb. can pineapple slices, drained)
1 green sweet pepper, deseeded and chopped
oil
salt
veal *or* chicken stock
1 teaspoon cornflour
2 tablespoons water
few drops sesame oil
1 teaspoon brandy
1 tablespoon soya sauce
1 teaspoon sugar
a few canned red cherries

Cut duck into thin slices; cut the pineapple into bite-sized pieces and reserve several for garnish.
Heat a little oil in a pan and add green pepper, pineapple. Season with salt, add stock to cover; cook for 1 minute. Add duck, cornflour blended with the water, sesame oil, brandy, soya sauce and sugar.
Cook for 4 minutes and serve garnished with reserved pineapple pieces and red cherries.

SHIU NGAP
CHINESE ROAST DUCK

Preparation time 15 minutes
Cooking time 1 hour
Oven temperature 218°C., 425°F., Gas Mark 7
To serve 6

You will need

5-lb. duck
salt
2 tablespoons brandy
2 teaspoons soya sauce
3 cloves garlic, crushed
1 oz. spring onions, chopped

Rub duck with salt. Mix 1 tablespoon brandy, 1 teaspoon soya sauce, half the garlic and half the spring onions. Put the mixture inside the duck, and sew up opening.
Turn on oven at temperature given above. Mix the rest of the ingredients together and rub some of the mixture all over the duck. Leave to stand until the mixture dries and repeat the rubbing process. Roast the duck for about 1 hour in the preheated oven, on a grid in the roasting pan. Add a little water to the pan and brush the duck with the remainder of the mixture every 15 minutes. Brown the bird well. Reduce the pan juices and serve as gravy with the duck.

PIGEON IN ORANGE PEEL SAUCE

Preparation time 5 minutes plus 15–20 minutes standing time
Cooking time 50–55 minutes
To serve 4

You will need

2 pieces dried orange peel
2 young pigeons, ready for cooking
4 tablespoons soya sauce
½ teaspoon fresh ginger, finely chopped
3 tablespoons Chinese wine *or* sherry
½ teaspoon sugar
salt
pepper
oil for deep frying
1¾ pints (U.S. 4¼ cups) chicken stock *or* water and stock cube
8–9 Chinese dried dates

Soak the orange peel in enough water to cover and leave until required.
Wash and dry the pigeons. In a small bowl mix soya sauce, ginger, wine, sugar and a pinch each of salt and pepper. Brush the pigeons with this mixture inside and outside. Leave for 15–20 minutes for the dressing to impregnate the birds. Then heat the oil, deep-fry the pigeons until golden. Remove, drain and put in a deep casserole.
Drain and shred orange peel, and add to pigeons with stock and dates. Simmer for 45–50 minutes and serve hot.

HAR YEN SAM SEE NGAP
DUCK WITH PRAWNS AND BAMBOO SHOOTS

Preparation time 10 minutes
Cooking time 2 hours 12 minutes
To serve 6

You will need

5-lb. duck and giblets
1 teaspoon salt
1 tablespoon soya sauce
1 tablespoon brandy
1 teaspoon cinnamon
2 oz. bamboo shoots
1 tablespoon oil
1 clove garlic, crushed
8 oz. prawns, peeled
8 oz. fresh mushrooms, sliced
2 pints (U.S. 5 cups) water
1 teaspoon cornflour

Clean and wash the duck, reserving giblets; rub bird with salt. Combine soya sauce, brandy and cinnamon and brush the duck with this mixture. Slice the giblets and bamboo shoots. Heat oil with garlic in a large pan, put in duck and giblets, fry until brown. Add prawns, bamboo shoots, mushrooms and the rest of the mixture used for brushing the duck. Add water, simmer gently for 2 hours, then add cornflour blended with 2 tablespoons cold water. Reheat and serve.

MEAT

GU LO YUK
SWEET AND SOUR PORK

(Illustrated in colour on page 87)

Preparation time 15 minutes
Cooking time 12 minutes
To serve 4

You will need

1 lb. pork (lean and fat)
salt
1 egg, beaten
cornflour for coating
lard or oil for deep frying

SWEET AND SOUR SAUCE
½ green sweet pepper, deseeded and chopped
½ red sweet pepper, deseeded and chopped
½ medium onion, skinned and chopped
oil
pinch ground green ginger
2 tablespoons vinegar
4 teaspoons sugar
2 teaspoons tomato sauce
2 teaspoons cornflour
1½ teaspoons soya sauce
1 teaspoon brandy
½ pint (U.S. 1¼ cups) water

Skin the pork, and cut into 1-inch cubes; season with salt. Dip cubes into beaten egg, then into cornflour. Deep-fry in lard or oil. The pork is cooked when it rises to the surface and acquires a lovely golden colour. Heap on a dish, and serve covered with sweet and sour sauce prepared in the following manner:
Fry the peppers and onion in a very little oil sprinkled with ginger. Mix together the vinegar, sugar, tomato sauce, 2 teaspoons cornflour, the soya sauce and brandy. Stir well, blend in the water, and add mixture to the fried vegetables. Simmer gently for 5 minutes, stirring all the time. If the sauce becomes too thick, add a little more water. Pour this sauce over the pork.

GEE YUK JING DAN
PORK OMELETTE

Preparation time 7 minutes
Cooking time 7 minutes
To serve 4

You will need

6 oz. lean pork
1 small onion
6 eggs
salt and pepper

Mince the pork, and chop the onion finely. Heat a large greased frying pan, and cook the onion for 30 seconds. Add minced pork, and cook, stirring, for 5 minutes. Beat eggs, season with salt and pepper, add to the pan, and cook until eggs begin to set, shaking the pan from time to time. Serve at once.

HO YOW NGOW YUK
STEAK WITH OYSTER SAUCE

Preparation time 15 minutes
Cooking time 4 minutes
To serve 4

You will need

12 oz. rump steak
1 knob green ginger
1 tablespoon soya sauce
1 tablespoon brandy
1 tablespoon cornflour
pinch salt
1 tablespoon oil
1 clove garlic, crushed
1 tablespoon oyster sauce
¼ pint (U.S. ⅔ cup) water

Slice meat wafer thin, and pound the ginger. Mix meat with ginger, soya sauce, brandy, cornflour and salt.
Heat oil in a pan with garlic until garlic browns. Add meat, stirring very briskly for 2 minutes. Add oyster sauce, and continue to cook quickly, stirring all the time, for 1 minute. Add water, cook for 30 seconds, and serve.

LIEN TZU NGOW YUK
FORMOSAN BEEF WITH LOTUS ROOTS

Preparation time 12 minutes
Cooking time 2 hours 13 minutes
To serve 4

You will need

1 lb. beef
1 clove garlic
1 oz. fresh ginger
cooking oil
salt
few drops oil of aniseed
1 teaspoon thick sweet sauce (available in cans)
1 small piece dried orange peel
soya sauce
4 oz. dried lotus roots
veal or beef stock

Cut beef into uniform pieces. Pound garlic and ginger separately. Put garlic in a hot, oiled pan, cook for a few minutes and remove. Place beef in pan, add salt to taste, and 'scramble' (i.e. cook quickly, stirring frequently) for 5 minutes. Add aniseed oil, ginger, thick sweet sauce and orange peel. Simmer for 5 minutes. Add a little soya sauce, the lotus roots, and sufficient veal or beef stock to cover. Cook slowly for 2 hours and serve.

GUNG PIN JEOU
GINGER-FLAVOURED SHERRY

Preparation time 10 minutes plus 12 hours standing time
Cooking time nil

Cut 1–2 oz. fresh ginger into thin strips. Turn them into a bottle and cover with a warm brown sherry. Leave to infuse, strain and use as directed. For 2 oz. fresh ginger, ½ bottle sherry will be the right amount to add.

DESSERT

LI TZU CHIANG
GINGER PEARS WITH LYCHEES

(Illustrated in colour on page 90)

Preparation time 7–13 minutes
Cooking time 5 minutes
To serve 4–6

You will need

15-oz. can pear halves
3–4 pieces preserved ginger in syrup
12 fresh lychees *or* 11-oz. can of lychees
2 bananas
little fresh coconut, grated (optional)

Drain the pears, reserving juice. Put the pear juice and 2 tablespoons of ginger syrup into a saucepan and boil rapidly to reduce by half. Cool. Slice ginger. Skin, halve and stone the lychees, or drain canned lychees. Peel and slice bananas thinly.
Arrange the bananas, pears and ginger in serving dish. Pour the cooled syrup over. Top with lychees. Decorate with slivers of ginger, and grated coconut if liked. Serve chilled.

Pork and pineapple (see recipe page 114) and, behind, hot fish sauce (see recipe page 112)

Gala salad

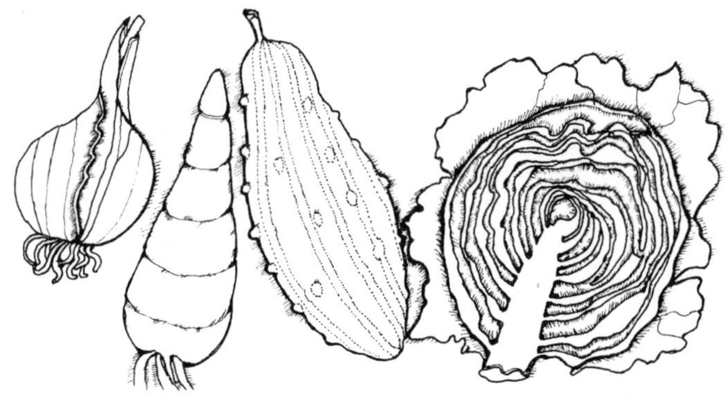

THAILAND

In Thailand rice is served with most meals along with soups, curries and vegetables. Several curries may be served at a meal and most Thai dishes are well spiced. Their presentation is of great importance and the same degree of attention to detail is given to the arrangement as to the preparation of food as can be seen from the illustrations.

The Gala Salad (see opposite) with a variety of colourful vegetables artistically cut and arranged is particularly attractive.

We were extremely fortunate in obtaining permission from the Royal Thai Embassy in Singapore to photograph the majority of Thai dishes which illustrate this chapter. They were part of a banquet given to celebrate the King of Thailand's birthday.

PAK SOD
GALA SALAD

(Illustrated in colour opposite)

This is a selection of as many different coloured vegetables as possible in season, made into an attractive salad dish. The vegetables should be as fresh as possible. The whole idea is to make a colourful picture as a focal point for the dining table.

Follow the pattern of the picture opposite, and slice radishes, spring onions, carrots, chillis and onions towards the stem end, keeping them whole; put them into iced water so that they open up. Build a display using lettuce leaves and sliced cabbage as a base, adding sliced vegetables as you wish, rather like a floral arrangement.

KHAO PLAW
BOILED RICE

Preparation time 1 minute
Cooking time about 30 minutes
To serve 5–6

You will need

$1\frac{3}{4}$ lb. rice
$\frac{1}{2}$ teaspoon salt
$2\frac{1}{2}$ pints (U.S. $6\frac{1}{4}$ cups) water

Wash the rice thoroughly, drain well. Put in pan and season with salt. Add water and bring to the boil. With a skimmer remove any scum which rises to the surface, boil for 10 minutes, then cover with a well-fitting lid. Reduce heat to the minimum and simmer for 18–20 minutes, by which time all the water should be absorbed.

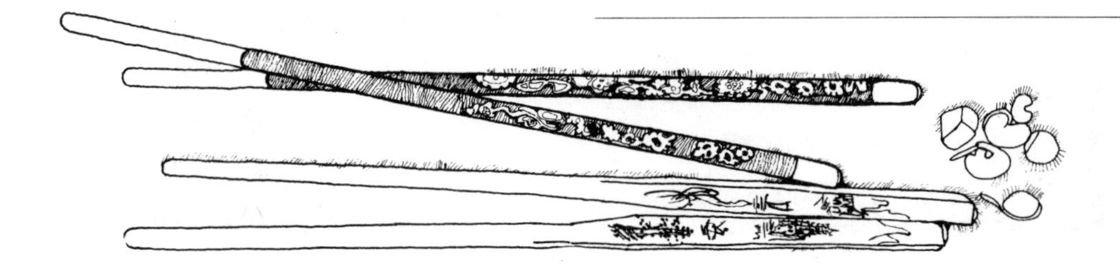

KAENG CHUD KUNG
PRAWN SOUP

Preparation time 15 minutes
Cooking time about 25 minutes
To serve 4

You will need

1 lb. peeled prawns
1 tablespoon lemon juice
1 teaspoon grated lemon rind
1 clove garlic
4 tablespoons finely chopped onions
2 teaspoons anchovy paste
pinch sugar
$\frac{1}{4}$ teaspoon black pepper
$\frac{1}{2}$ teaspoon salt
small pinch ground coriander
$\frac{1}{4}$ teaspoon chilli powder
2 teaspoons soya sauce
$1\frac{1}{2}$ pints (U.S. $3\frac{3}{4}$ cups) coconut milk (see page 53)

Chop the prawns, sprinkle with lemon juice and rind. Pound the garlic, onions, anchovy paste, sugar, pepper, salt, coriander, chilli powder and soya sauce in a mortar. Put this mixture in a pan, gradually blend with coconut milk and heat slowly. Simmer on lowest possible heat for 15 minutes.
Add prawns, stir, simmer for 6–7 minutes and serve.

KAENG CHUD KUB KAI
CHICKEN AND MUSHROOM SOUP

(Illustrated in black and white below)

Preparation time 15 minutes
Cooking time about 1 hour
To serve 6

You will need

$2\frac{1}{2}$-lb. chicken
6 oz. button mushrooms
2–3 cloves garlic
1 teaspoon ground coriander
$\frac{3}{4}$ teaspoon pepper
2 tablespoons chicken fat
salt
1 tablespoon sugar (palm sugar, if available)

Cook the chicken in $3\frac{1}{2}$ pints (U.S. 9 cups) water, until tender. Take the flesh off the bones and slice. Return the bones to the stock and simmer until stock is reduced by half.
Bring the mushrooms to the boil in enough water to cover, cook for 2 minutes and drain.
Pound the garlic, coriander and pepper to a paste. Heat chicken fat and fry the paste in it for 3 minutes, stirring all the time.
Add the chicken and cook, stirring, for 2 minutes. Season with salt to taste, sprinkle with sugar and pour in strained stock. Bring to the boil, add mushrooms, cover and simmer for 5 minutes.

Chicken and mushroom soup

MI KROB
FRIED NOODLES
(Illustrated in colour on page 117)

Preparation time	10 minutes plus 30 minutes standing time
Cooking time	30–35 minutes
To serve	4–6

You will need

1 lb. Chinese rice noodles
1 medium onion
3–4 cloves garlic
6 oz. uncooked lean pork
8 oz. uncooked chicken meat
4 oz. crab meat
8 oz. uncooked prawns
1 square bean curd
4–6 oz. bean sprouts
½ pint (U.S. 1¼ cups) oil for frying
1 tablespoon soya sauce
1 tablespoon vinegar
1 tablespoon anchovy paste
1 tablespoon sugar
salt
3–4 spring onions
4 eggs
few coriander leaves
2 red chillis, deseeded and sliced (optional)

Break the noodles into pieces and drop into boiling salted water. Simmer for 1 minute, drain well and spread on a dish. Leave to dry for 30 minutes.
Chop onion and garlic. Slice pork and chicken meat. Flake crab meat. Peel, de-vein and chop prawns. Cut bean curd into small dice. Wash and drain bean sprouts.
Reserving 2 tablespoons of oil, heat rest in a deep frying pan and fry the noodles until crisp and pale golden, turning twice. Remove, drain thoroughly and leave aside.
Heat remaining oil in a frying pan and lightly fry onion and garlic. Add pork and cook for 8–10 minutes, stirring frequently. Add chicken, cook stirring for 3 minutes. Add crab meat, prawns and bean curd, cook stirring for a few minutes until the chicken and prawns change colour. Season with the soya sauce, vinegar, anchovy paste, sugar, and salt to taste. Mix well, simmer on low heat for 5 minutes. Chop spring onions. Beat eggs and pour into the pan, stir to mix. As soon as eggs begin to set, add bean sprouts and noodles, cook stirring for a couple of minutes to heat through. Transfer to a heated serving dish, sprinkle with spring onions and coriander, garnish with red chillis, if liked, and serve.

YUM KUNG
LOBSTER SALAD

Preparation time	20 minutes
Cooking time	24–26 minutes
To serve	4

You will need

2 small lobsters
salt
bay leaf
2 green sweet peppers
1–2 tablespoons peanut oil
1 clove garlic, finely chopped
3–4 shallots, finely chopped
1 peach, peeled and thinly sliced
1 tablespoon soya sauce
2 tablespoons chopped peanuts
¼ pint (U.S. ⅔ cup) coconut milk (see page 53)

Cook the lobsters in boiling water, with salt and bay leaf. Make sure you have enough water to immerse the lobsters completely. Allow 18–20 minutes cooking time. It is important to time the boiling correctly; overcooking ruins the texture of the meat and makes it tough, insufficient cooking prevents the coral turning red.
Drain the lobsters, cut each in half, remove little bag from head and the black intestinal line. Remove meat from shell, cut into bite-sized pieces. Arrange on a serving dish. Cut the peppers in half, remove seeds and rinse. Drop into boiling water for 1 minute, drain and cut into shreds. Heat the oil and fry garlic and shallots until transparent.
Allow to cool. Add peach, soya sauce, peanuts and coconut milk. Stir, spread the mixture over lobster, sprinkle with shredded green pepper and serve cold.

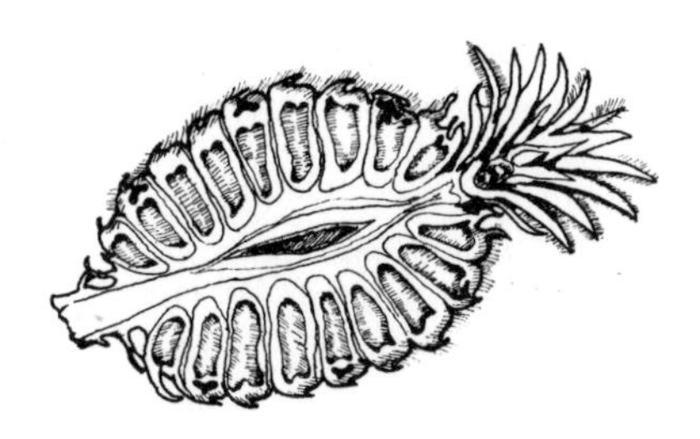

Fried fish

PLA THOO
FRIED FISH
(Illustrated in black and white above)

The fish which is normally used in Thailand for this dish, as shown in the illustration, is found only in the Bay of Siam. Trout, mackerel or herring are all good substitutes.

Preparation time 10 minutes
Cooking time 10 minutes
To serve 4

You will need

4 fresh trout
pinch turmeric
1 teaspoon gros sel *or* sea salt
6 tablespoons oil
nam prik (see right)

Gut and clean each trout well, under running water if possible; dry on a cloth. Pound or grind the turmeric with the salt and rub the mixture into the fish.
Heat the oil in a frying pan and fry 2 at a time in hot oil until golden on both sides. Do not overcook. Drain well and serve at once. Serve nam prik in a separate dish.

NAM PRIK
HOT FISH SAUCE
(Illustrated in colour on page 117)

Found on every Thai dining-table, this sauce is served with practically everything except sweet dishes. Like nam pla the flavour is strong and tends to smother other foods, so use with discretion!

Preparation time 20 minutes
Cooking time nil

You will need

2 tablespoons salted fish *or* dried, salted shrimps
6 cloves garlic
pinch brown sugar
1 tablespoon nam pla (see below)
fresh red chillis to taste, deseeded and chopped
3 tablespoons lime *or* lemon juice
2 teaspoons soya sauce

Pound fish or shrimps, garlic, sugar, nam pla and chillis in a mortar until smooth. Gradually add lime or lemon juice and soya sauce and mix in well. Alternatively put everything through a blender, though this would make the sauce too smooth for Thai taste.
Garnish with red and green chillis, if liked.

NAM PLA
FISH SAUCE

This is a fish sauce, very popular with most Thai people and used a great deal in cooking. Its flavour is very pungent and not usually liked by people who are not used to it. It is sold in shops specialising in oriental produce. However here is a slightly westernised version.

Preparation time 10 minutes
Cooking time nil

You will need

6 anchovy fillets
1 clove garlic, chopped
½ teaspoon soya sauce

Pound all ingredients thoroughly until they are a smooth paste. This amount will make about 2 tablespoons. Use as required.

SOM TAM
PAPAYA SALAD
(Illustrated in colour on page 117)

Preparation time 15 minutes
Cooking time nil
To serve 4

You will need

1 crisp lettuce
8 oz. white cabbage, shredded
half a papaya *or* 2 peaches, peeled and sliced
2–3 firm tomatoes, peeled and sliced
$1\frac{1}{2}$ tablespoons lime *or* lemon juice
1 tablespoon nam pla (see page 112)
3 teaspoons finely chopped spring onions
fresh red chillis to taste, split and deseeded
1 tablespoon roasted chopped peanuts (optional)
2 tablespoons salted dried shrimps *or* potted shrimps (optional)

Wash the lettuce and arrange on a dish. Garnish with the cabbage, fruit and tomato slices. Mix the lemon or lime juice with the nam pla and spring onions and use as a salad dressing, either mixing it with the salad, or serving it separately. Just before serving, garnish salad with chillis, and peanuts and shrimps if liked.

MOO PAD NAW MAI
PORK CASSEROLE
(Illustrated in black and white below)

Preparation time 5 minutes
Cooking time 30 minutes
To serve 4–6

You will need

1 lb. bamboo shoots, sliced
salt
$1\frac{1}{2}$ lb. pork, cut in large dice
5–6 cloves garlic
$\frac{1}{2}$ teaspoon ground coriander
generous $\frac{1}{2}$ pint (U.S. $1\frac{1}{2}$ cups) chicken stock *or* water with a stock cube
$\frac{1}{2}$ teaspoon pepper
1 tablespoon sugar

If fresh bamboo shoots are used, slice them, bring to the boil in salted water and simmer until they turn pale yellow. Drain immediately.
Canned bamboo shoots usually need no preliminary cooking, unless specified on the can.
Fry the pork in a pan without any fat (it yields enough of its own fat) and stir to brown evenly. Pound the garlic with coriander and stir into the pork. Add bamboo shoots and enough stock to cover. Season to taste with salt and pepper. Sprinkle with sugar, stir, cover and cook slowly until the pork is tender – about 20 minutes.

Pork casserole

MA HUO
PORK AND PINEAPPLE

(Illustrated in colour on page 107)

Preparation time 10 minutes plus 30 minutes cooling time
Cooking time 16–17 minutes
To serve 4

You will need

12 oz. uncooked lean pork
1 clove garlic
1 tablespoon peanut oil
2 oz. peanuts
1 teaspoon anchovy paste
pinch ground coriander
$\frac{1}{4}$ teaspoon chilli powder
salt
fresh pineapple, peeled, cored and cut into large chunks
fresh coriander leaves
fresh red chillis, deseeded and cut into thin strips

Mince the pork. Chop the garlic finely. Heat oil, fry garlic for 1–2 minutes. Add pork and cook stirring for 5 minutes. Chop peanuts, add to pork, together with anchovy paste, coriander and chillis. Reduce heat and simmer, stirring frequently for 10 minutes. Season with salt to taste. Cool. Divide the meat among the pineapple chunks and garnish with coriander leaves and chilli strips.

MOO PESES
PORK AND ONION

Preparation time 10 minutes
Cooking time 40–45 minutes
To serve 4

You will need

generous $\frac{1}{4}$ pint (U.S. $\frac{3}{4}$ cup) stock
1 teaspoon finely sliced ginger
1 lb. lean pork, cut in large dice
6 oz. onion, chopped
2 cloves garlic, chopped
2 tablespoons oil
salt
pinch chilli powder

Bring the stock to the boil with the ginger, simmer for 5 minutes and remove from heat.
Fry the pork with half the onion and 1 clove garlic in oil, until brown. Season with salt and chilli powder to taste. Add stock, simmer for 15 minutes and remove from heat.
Remove the pork with a perforated spoon; chop or mince with the rest of the onion and garlic. Put back in the sauce, simmer for another 15–20 minutes and serve with rice.

KAI KUB KAO-LAD
CHICKEN WITH CHESTNUTS

Preparation time 15 minutes
Cooking time 1 hour 55 minutes
To serve 4

You will need

1 lb. uncooked chicken joints
giblets from 1 chicken
3–4 cloves garlic
$\frac{1}{2}$ teaspoon ground coriander
$\frac{1}{2}$ teaspoon pepper
2 tablespoons lard
1 lb. chestnuts, boiled and peeled
salt
1 tablespoon sugar (palm sugar, if available)

Remove the bones from the chicken, cut the flesh into pieces. Put the bones and trimmings in a small pan, cover with water, bring to the boil, cover, and simmer for 1 hour to make stock.
Slice the giblets.
Pound to a paste in a mortar the garlic, coriander and pepper. Heat the lard and fry the paste for 2–3 minutes, stirring all the time. Add the chicken and cook, stirring, until all the pieces change colour. Strain the stock on to the chicken mixture and bring to the boil. Add giblets, cook for 5 minutes. Put in chestnuts, season with salt and sprinkle in the sugar. Cover and simmer for about 45 minutes or until the chicken is tender.

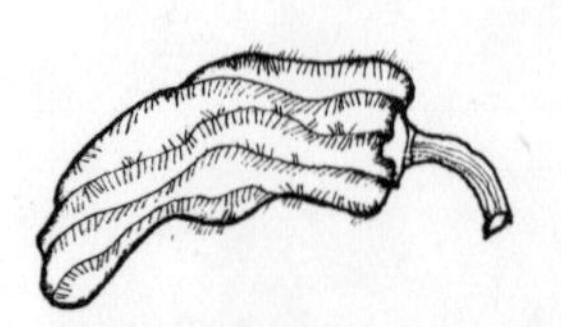

KAENG PHED
RED CURRY
(Illustrated in colour on page 118)

This dish can be made with beef or chicken. It is called red because of its garnish of red chillis.

Preparation time 20 minutes
Cooking time 35–40 minutes
To serve 6

You will need

3-lb. chicken *or* 2 lb. tender steak
2 pints (U.S. 5 cups) coconut cream (see page 53)
6–8 dried chillis, deseeded and chopped
2–3 oz. white cabbage, shredded
2 tablespoons finely chopped shallots
2 tablespoons finely chopped garlic
1 teaspoon salt
1 teaspoon peppercorns
1 teaspoon caraway seeds
1 teaspoon coriander seeds
½ teaspoon dried basil
1 teaspoon grated lemon rind
1½–2 tablespoons nam pla (see page 112)
8–12 fresh red chillis

Joint the chicken (or cut beef into strips about 1 inch thick and 3 inches long).
Bring half the coconut cream gently to the boil. Add meat, cover and simmer over lowest possible heat for 20–25 minutes.
Pound together the dried chillis, cabbage, shallots, garlic, salt, peppercorns, caraway, coriander, basil and lemon rind until smooth. The resulting curry paste is called kaeng phed. Add this to the simmering chicken or beef. Stir well. Add remaining coconut cream. Blend in nam pla. Continue to simmer for another 10 minutes.
Wash, dry and split the fresh chillis. Remove the seeds. Add chillis to curry. Simmer gently for 5 minutes. In Thailand, extra chillis would be used for garnish together with other fresh spices.

NEUA KUB NAM MAPRAW
BEEF IN COCONUT MILK

Strips of beef cooked in coconut milk, served on a bed of lightly cooked spinach, dressed with yoghourt and served with rice. Veal or chicken can be prepared in the same manner.

Preparation time 10 minutes
Cooking time 12–13 minutes
To serve 6

You will need

1½ pints (U.S. 3¾ cups) coconut milk (see page 53)
1½ lb. lean beef, cut into thin strips
1 oz. roasted peanuts, finely chopped
5 teaspoons soya sauce
1 tablespoon brown sugar
6 spring onions, chopped
2 cloves garlic, chopped
2–3 slices fresh ginger
2–3 dried red chillis (more if you want the sauce really hot)
salt
1 teaspoon cornflour
2 tablespoons cold water
1½ lb. spinach, lightly cooked in salted water and well drained
½ pint (U.S. 1¼ cups) yoghourt

Reserve generous ¼ pint (U.S. ¾ cup) coconut milk. Add rest to beef strips in a pan. Gently bring to the boil, simmer for 5 minutes. Add peanuts, soya sauce and sugar. Pound the spring onions, garlic, ginger and chillis with a pinch of salt, gradually adding the reserved coconut milk. Mix well and add to pan. Simmer for 2–3 minutes. Blend the cornflour with water and stir into the pan. Simmer, stirring, until the sauce thickens. Check seasoning.
Have the cooked spinach ready in a heated serving dish. Spoon the beef and sauce over it. Top with yoghourt and serve.

KLUAY CHUAM
BANANAS WITH COCONUT CREAM

Preparation time 2–3 minutes
Cooking time 10 minutes
To serve 6

You will need

4 oz. sugar
scant ½ pint (U.S. 1 cup) water
6 firm but ripe bananas
½ pint (U.S. 1¼ cups) thick coconut cream (see page 53)
small pinch salt

Slowly melt the sugar with the water over a gentle heat and bring to the boil. Peel the bananas and cut into chunks. Drop them into the boiling syrup. Simmer, skimming off any scum which rises to the surface, until the bananas are well glazed and the syrup reaches 'thread' stage. To test, touch the surface of the syrup with a spoon. If the syrup forms a fibrous thread, it is ready. Or, if you use a sugar thermometer, this stage is reached at 219°F. (104°C). Whisk coconut cream lightly with a pinch of salt.
Transfer bananas and syrup to a serving dish and serve with coconut cream.

KLUAY TOD LAD NAM CHUAM
CARAMELISED BANANA SLICES

Preparation time 5 minutes
Cooking time 10 minutes
To serve 4

You will need

4 firm but ripe bananas
lime *or* lemon juice
peanut oil for deep frying
6 tablespoons sugar
3 tablespoons water

Peel bananas, slice thinly, sprinkle with lime or lemon juice and leave to stand. Meanwhile heat the oil and prepare caramel syrup.
To make the syrup: slowly melt the sugar in the water, then increase heat and let it boil until it turns pale caramel colour – do not allow it to brown. As soon as the syrup is ready, remove the pan from the heat and stand it on a dish cloth, dipped in cold water and wrung out.
Deep-fry the banana slices in the hot oil, a few at a time, for a few seconds. Remove with a perforated spoon to a heated metal dish. Continue in this manner until all slices are fried and laid on the dish, which should be big enough to take them in a single layer.
Reheat the syrup and pour it over the bananas in an even trickle so that it coats all the slices.
Serve at once.
Provide each guest with a bowl of iced water for dipping banana slices before eating. This hardens the caramel.

FOI TONG
THAI SILK

(Illustrated in colour opposite)

Preparation time 5 minutes
Cooking time 7–8 minutes
To serve 4

You will need

10 oz. sugar
scant ½ pint (U.S. 1 cup) water
1 teaspoon jasmine (or other blossom) water
8 egg yolks, lightly beaten

Slowly bring sugar, water and jasmine water to the boil, simmer gently until the syrup thickens. Using an icing bag with a small nozzle, or a funnel, pour the yolks into the syrup in a thin, thread-like trickle and spiral them into little pyramids. As soon as these set, carefully remove to a heated serving dish. Cook a few at a time and keep warm until all the egg yolk has been used up.
The name Foi Tong means literally 'strings of gold'. The little 'spools' are piled into a wy, a narrow pyramid, resembling the hands put together for a traditional Thai greeting.

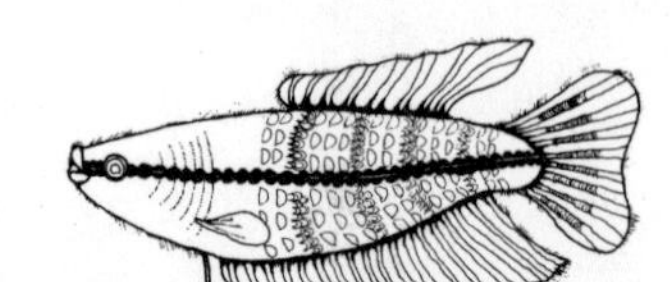

From back, left to right: Thai silk (see recipe page 116), hot fish sauce (see recipe page 112), fried noodles (see recipe page 111), papaya salad (see recipe page 113)

Red curry (see recipe page 115)

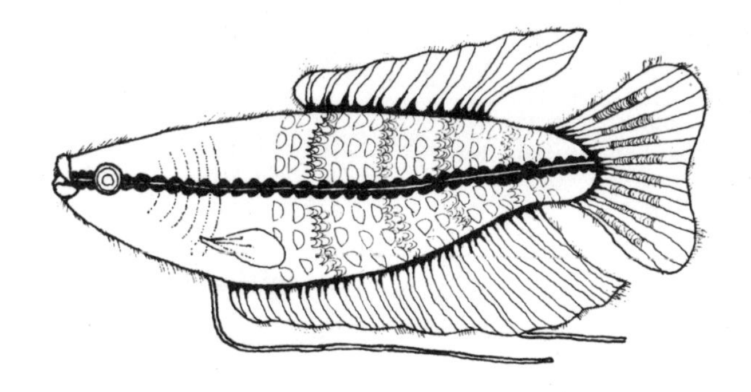

MALAYSIA AND SINGAPORE

Malaysian cooks are exceptionally clever at preparing both sea and fresh-water fish. Another skill they have perfected is the making of non-alcoholic 'cocktails', since, being predominantly Moslems, their religion forbids the drinking of alcohol. Pomegranate and tamarind juice, fresh coconut and sugar cane juice, mango and fresh ginger, carambola, and other local fruit are used to produce attractive drinks with names like Orchid Swizzle and Angel's Delight, but as this is a cookery book I have not given any recipes for drinks!
Singapore is a great melting pot of all Asian cuisines. There are eating places to suit every taste and pocket. Street vendors sell sizzling satay and neat packages of rice steamed in little square 'baskets'. Huge piles of fresh banana leaves are stacked on pavements, like bales of hay. There are many restaurants of Asian haute cuisine, with prices to match, and kerb-side portable kitchens, filling the air with tantalising smells. A bleak day-time car park is at night transformed into an open-air Chinese food fair, with scores of stall-kitchens, each specialising in one or two dishes. The regulars make a meal sampling a morsel or two from a dozen stalls. I was taken on such a 'stall crawl' by three charming young people and the experience was unforgettable.

MALAYSIA

TĔRONG
CURRIED AUBERGINES

Preparation time 15 minutes plus 10–15 minutes standing time
Cooking time 37 minutes
To serve 6

You will need

2 lb. aubergines
salt
2–3 tablespoons peanut oil
3 medium onions, finely sliced
2 cloves garlic, chopped
1 tablespoon curry powder
2 green sweet peppers, deseeded and sliced
1–2 deseeded dried chillis, pounded (optional)
small pinch dry mustard
¼ pint (U.S. ⅔ cup) coconut milk (see page 53)

Wash the aubergines, remove stem, but do not peel. Cut in cubes, sprinkle with salt and leave to stand for 10–15 minutes. Pour off the juice. Rinse well and dry in a clean tea towel.
Heat the oil and fry the onions and garlic until the onions become transparent and soft.
Stir in the curry powder. Add the aubergine cubes and fry, stirring carefully, for 1 minute.
Add peppers and chillis, if used. Check seasoning, add more salt, if necessary, and the mustard. Moisten with the coconut milk, cover, reduce heat and simmer gently for 30 minutes.

CLARIFIED BUTTER

Melt butter on a very low heat until it begins to look like olive oil and a whitish deposit forms on the bottom of the pan. To get rid of the sediment, strain into a clean jar.

LAKSA LEMAK
EGG NOODLES WITH PRAWNS
(Illustrated in black and white below)

This is a Malaysian dish of egg noodles, served with prawns, garnished with chillis, cucumber and kesom or basil leaves.

Preparation time 10 minutes
Cooking time 20 minutes
To serve 4

You will need

8 oz. laksa (noodles)
salt
6 oz. onion, chopped
1 clove garlic
2 tablespoons cashew nuts or almonds
pinch saffron *or* turmeric
1 tablespoon shredded fresh ginger
2 teaspoons blachan (Malaysian prawn paste) *or* anchovy paste
3–4 tablespoons oil
1 lb. cooked peeled prawns
1 pint (U.S. $2\frac{1}{2}$ cups) coconut milk (see page 53)
3 tablespoons cucumber sliced into matchstick strips (julienne)
shredded kesom *or* basil leaves
red and green chillis

Boil the noodles in salted water.
Meanwhile, start making the prawn sauce. In a mortar pound the onion, garlic, nuts, saffron or turmeric, ginger and blachan. Heat the oil and cook the pounded mixture for 2–3 minutes, stirring all the time. Add the prawns, stir, and cook for 1 minute. Season with salt to taste, reduce the heat and blend in the coconut milk. Stir, simmer for a few minutes, cover and keep hot, but do not allow to boil.
Drain the noodles, arrange on a heated serving dish and pour the prawns and the sauce over them. Garnish with cucumber slices and sprinkle with kesom or basil leaves. Serve a dish of chillis separately.

Note
So that they can be seen clearly, garnishes are shown on side dishes in the picture right.

UDANG MASAK LEMAK
PRAWNS IN COCONUT
(Illustrated in black and white on page 122)

Preparation time 10 minutes
Cooking time 18 minutes
To serve 4

You will need

2 large onions, chopped
2–3 tablespoons ghee *or* clarified butter (see page 119)
1 teaspoon curry powder
2 dried red chillis, deseeded and chopped
1 green sweet pepper, deseeded and sliced
12 large prawns, boiled
salt
$\frac{1}{2}$ pint (U.S. $1\frac{1}{4}$ cups) coconut cream (see page 53)

Brown the onions lightly in the fat. Stir in the curry powder and cook together, stirring all the time, for 3 minutes. Add chillis and green pepper, cover and simmer over a low heat for 10 minutes. Add the prawns, season with salt to taste, mix well and cook for 1 minute. Reduce heat, add the coconut cream and simmer gently to heat through. On no account allow the sauce to boil after you have added the coconut cream.
Serve with plain boiled rice.

Egg noodles with prawns

Fish in coconut milk (1)

FISH MOOLIE
FISH IN COCONUT MILK *1*
(Illustrated in black and white above)

To be authentic, this dish requires certain varieties of fish known by their Malaysian names as ikan merah, tenggiri or kurau, which are not available in Europe. But, just as bouillabaise is made and eaten in many parts of the world, although its essential ingredient, rascasse, cannot be obtained outside the Mediterranean area, cooks have learned to make acceptable versions of moolie by using substitutes. In fact any good quality white-fleshed fish is suitable.

Preparation time 5 minutes
Cooking time 17–20 minutes
To serve 4

You will need

1½ lb. white fish
ghee *or* oil
1 red chilli, deseeded
1 tablespoon shredded fresh ginger
8 oz. shallots, sliced
1 teaspoon turmeric
salt
½ pint (U.S. 1¼ cups) coconut cream (see page 53)
½ pint (U.S. 1¼ cups) coconut milk (see page 53)
crisp fried onion rings
red and green chillis

Keep fish whole, clean, wipe and brown lightly in 1–2 tablespoons fat. Remove from pan. Add another tablespoon fat to the pan and fry red deseeded chilli, ginger and shallots, stirring, for 3–4 minutes. Sprinkle in the turmeric and salt to taste.
Reduce heat and carefully blend in half the coconut cream and all the coconut milk. Add fish and simmer on the lowest possible heat for 8–10 minutes, testing the fish from time to time to see if it is cooked. Add remaining coconut cream and check seasoning.
Reheat, garnish with the fried onion rings and red and green chillis. Serve with fresh limes and boiled rice.

AJAM PANGGANG
CHICKEN WITH GREEN CHILLIS

Preparation time 15 minutes
Cooking time 44 minutes
To serve 4–6

You will need

3 tablespoons butter
1 large onion, finely chopped
2 cloves garlic, chopped
3½-lb. chicken, jointed
1 knob green ginger, pounded
salt
juice of 1 lime *or* lemon
¼ pint (U.S. ⅔ cup) water
½ teaspoon turmeric
4–5 green chillis, deseeded and diced

Heat the butter and fry the onion and garlic until soft. Add the chicken and brown lightly on all sides. Sprinkle with the ginger and salt. Cover and simmer slowly for 20 minutes. Mix the lime juice with the water and add to chicken. Stir in the turmeric, then add chillis and continue to simmer until the chicken is tender – about 15 minutes. Serve with plain boiled rice.

OTAK OTAK
FISH ROLLS
(Illustrated in colour on page 128)

Preparation time 5 minutes
Cooking time 42–48 minutes
Oven temperature 177°C., 350°F., Gas Mark 4
To serve 4

You will need

1 lb. firm, white-fleshed fish fillets, minced
1 oz. coconut, grated
3 tablespoons cooking oil
4 oz. onion, chopped
2 eggs, lightly beaten
½ tablespoon curry powder
2 tablespoons chopped cashew nuts *or* almonds
pinch salt
1 clove garlic, finely chopped
⅛ pint (U.S. ⅓ cup) coconut milk (see page 53)
4 banana leaves or pieces of foil cut into four 8-inch squares

Make sure the fish is thoroughly boned, skinned and finely minced.
Turn on oven at temperature given above.
Fry the coconut in half the oil for 2–3 minutes and remove from the heat.
Fry the onion in the remaining oil until soft and pale golden. Mix fish, coconut, onion and the rest of the ingredients (except banana leaves) and stir well.
Lightly grease the banana leaves or foil and divide the mixture among them. Wrap up, secure with cocktail sticks and bake in the preheated oven for 35–40 minutes.

PANGGANG PERCHIK
MARINATED STEAKS

Preparation time 15 minutes plus 2 hours 30 minutes – 3 hours standing time
Cooking time 5–10 minutes
To serve 4

You will need

4 small beef steaks
2 fresh chillis
2 medium onions, chopped
1 piece root ginger, sliced
2 teaspoons lime *or* lemon juice
salt
1 tablespoon brown sugar
pinch saffron
½ pint (U.S. 1¼ cups) coconut milk (see page 53)

Trim the steaks. Put the chillis, onions and ginger into a mortar, moisten with lime or lemon juice, and pound to a smooth paste. Add salt, sugar, saffron and coconut milk. Stir well. Put the steaks into a deep dish, pour the spiced coconut mixture over them and leave to marinate for 2½–3 hours, turning from time to time.
Remove the steaks and grill to taste, basting with the marinade. Arrange the cooked steaks on a dish and keep warm. Heat the spiced coconut liquid, strain over the meat, and serve.

Prawns in coconut (see recipe page 120)

Fish in coconut milk (2)

SATAY, MALAYSIAN STYLE

(Illustrated in colour on the front cover)

Preparation time 17 minutes
Cooking time 9 minutes
To serve 4

You will need

1 lb. beef fillet, cut in 1-inch cubes
salt and pepper
2 cloves garlic, finely chopped
1 tablespoon sugar
oil

FOR THE SAUCE

1 oz. butter
1 medium onion, finely chopped
juice of 1 lime *or* lemon
1 teaspoon soya sauce
2 tablespoons sugar

Season the meat with salt and pepper, sprinkle with garlic and 1 tablespoon sugar. Mix well and leave to stand for a few minutes while you prepare the sauce.
Heat butter and fry the onion until transparent. Add the lime or lemon juice, soya sauce and 2 tablespoons sugar. Mix well and reheat without boiling.
Put the beef cubes on lightly oiled skewers, dip in sauce then grill, basting frequently with the sauce.

SINGAPORE

MOOLIE

FISH IN COCONUT MILK 2

(Illustrated in black and white above)

Preparation time 7 minutes
Cooking time 13–18 minutes
To serve 4

You will need

1 lb. cod or haddock fillets
salt and pepper
2–3 dried chillis
pinch coriander
¼ teaspoon cumin
1 clove garlic
small piece tamarind, crushed
1 onion, chopped
¼ teaspoon turmeric
2 tablespoons oil
½ pint (U.S. 1¼ cups) coconut milk (see page 53)

Cut the fish into four pieces and season with salt and pepper. In a mortar, pound chillis, coriander, cumin, garlic, tamarind and onion, to make a curry paste. Add turmeric, blend well and fry the mixture in oil for a few minutes, stirring briskly. Add fish and coconut milk, simmer gently for 10–15 minutes and serve.

SINGAPORE PIGEON IN LETTUCE SHELLS WITH DEEP-FRIED NOODLES

Preparation time 15 minutes plus 30 minutes standing time
Cooking time 20 minutes
To serve 4–6

You will need

3 large dried mushrooms
2 young pigeons, boned
3 chicken livers
2½ pints (U.S. 6 cups) oil for deep frying
3 oz. rice noodles
1 egg yolk
salt and pepper
2 tablespoons butter *or* oil
3 oz. bamboo shoots, sliced
8–10 water chestnuts, chopped
1 green sweet pepper, deseeded and diced
6 spring onions, cut in ½-inch pieces
4–6 thin slices fresh ginger, chopped
1 tablespoon light soya sauce
1 teaspoon monosodium glutamate (optional)
1 teaspoon sugar
1 teaspoon sesame oil
lettuce leaf 'shells'

Soak mushrooms in water for at least 30 minutes, discard stalks, slice caps thinly and reserve. Mince the pigeons with the chicken livers.
Heat 2½ pints oil and deep-fry the noodles until golden. Drain on kitchen paper and set aside.
Mix minced pigeon and chicken livers with egg yolk, season with a pinch of salt and pepper. Quick-fry in the butter or oil, then lower heat and cook gently for 3 minutes.
Add mushrooms, bamboo shoots, water chestnuts, green pepper, spring onions and ginger. Cook together on medium heat for 10 minutes, stirring frequently.
Add soya sauce, monosodium glutamate, sugar, salt and pepper to taste, 1–2 tablespoons water and sesame oil. Simmer for 2 minutes.
Spoon a helping of the pigeon mixture into each crisp lettuce shell, surround with a border of fried noodles and serve.

SINGAPORE SATAY
SKEWERED MEAT CUBES

Another version of Satay – the Far East's answer to shashlik and kebab, but far daintier. Beef and pork are the most popular kinds of meat used. The sauce which accompanies it looks cool, but can be hot enough to set one's throat ablaze. I have, therefore, reduced the quantity of chillis used in the traditional recipe, and all you need to do to convert it back to its original ferocity is to multiply the number of chillis by at least four!
Satay is popular over a vast area, from Java to Hong Kong; it is served at elegant cocktail parties (cooked on small bamboo skewers, it can easily be handed round), popular restaurants and even on street corners. With the gentler type of satay sauce, frequently referred to as 'Java's secret', I find Satay irresistible.

Preparation time 15 minutes
Cooking time 37 minutes
To serve 4

You will need

1 small onion
1 clove garlic
8 oz. roasted peanuts
1–2 fresh chillis
1½ teaspoons brown sugar
juice of ½ lemon
½ pint (U.S. 1¼ cups) coconut milk (see page 53)
1 tablespoon soya sauce
1 lb. lean beef
salt
freshly ground black pepper

In a mortar pound the onion, garlic, peanuts, chillis and sugar to a smooth paste. Dry-fry for a moment, moisten with the lemon juice, add 4 tablespoons coconut milk and the soya sauce. Bring to the boil, then simmer gently for about 30 minutes to thicken the sauce. Cool, pour into a jar, and keep until needed. (This sauce keeps in a refrigerator for up to 1 month.)
Cut the meat into bite-sized cubes and season with salt and pepper. Impale on small skewers (preferably bamboo, as they do not burn), dip in remaining coconut milk, and grill in the usual manner, basting frequently with coconut milk. Serve with the satay sauce.

Curried chicken salad

Lontong chicken

CURRIED CHICKEN SALAD

(Illustrated in black and white above)

Preparation time 25 minutes
Cooking time nil
To serve 6–8

You will need

3½-lb. chicken, cooked
6 oz. cold cooked rice
2 oz. cooked peas
3 tablespoons French dressing (see page 126)
¼ pint (U.S. ⅔ cup) mayonnaise
2 teaspoons curry powder
3 tablespoons single cream
1 red sweet pepper, skinned, deseeded and sliced
1 stick celery, shredded
cabbage
2 tablespoons shredded coconut

Bone the chicken and dice the meat. Mix the rice with the cooked peas and toss in the dressing. Mix together the mayonnaise, curry powder and cream. Stir in the chicken, rice mixture, red pepper and celery. Arrange on crisp cabbage leaves, sprinkle with coconut and serve.

RENDAN LONTONG
LONTONG CHICKEN

(Illustrated in colour on page 127 and black and white above, right)

This is a variation on the Malaysian dish, Chicken with Green Chillis (see page 121). Follow ingredients and method as given, but leave the chicken whole and increase first cooking time given to 40 minutes. Omit green chillis and instead garnish with red chillis and a little cress.

IKAN MASAK LEMAK
HADDOCK DRY CURRY

Preparation time 10 minutes
Cooking time 15–16 minutes
To serve 4–6

You will need

1½ lb. haddock fillets, skinned
salt and pepper
2–3 dried chillis
6 peppercorns
small pinch cumin
1 clove garlic
½ teaspoon tamarind
2–3 shallots, finely chopped
¼ teaspoon turmeric
2 tablespoons oil
generous ¼ pint (U.S. ¾ cup) coconut milk (see page 53)

Cut the haddock into strips of a similar size. Season with salt and pepper. In a mortar, pound the remaining ingredients, except oil and coconut milk, to a smooth paste. Fry this paste in the oil for 4–5 minutes, stirring all the time. Reduce heat, add the fish, and cook for 30 seconds, stirring carefully. Add coconut milk and simmer, stirring constantly, for 10 minutes.

DUCK POACHED WITH TANGERINE PEEL

Preparation time 3 minutes
Cooking time 2 hours 30 minutes – 3 hours
To serve 6

You will need

5-lb. duck
3 pints (U.S. 7½ cups) water
2 oz. tangerine peel, dried
1 teaspoon ground ginger
2–3 spring onions, cut in 2-inch lengths
salt and pepper

Place all the ingredients together in a large saucepan. Simmer slowly, covered, for 2½–3 hours, until the duck is tender. Drain. Serve, seasoned with salt and pepper to taste.

FRENCH DRESSING

Preparation time 5 minutes
Cooking time nil

You will need

oil
vinegar
salt and pepper

Mix 3 parts of oil to 1 part vinegar, with salt and pepper to taste. Lemon juice may be used instead of vinegar. Use as required.

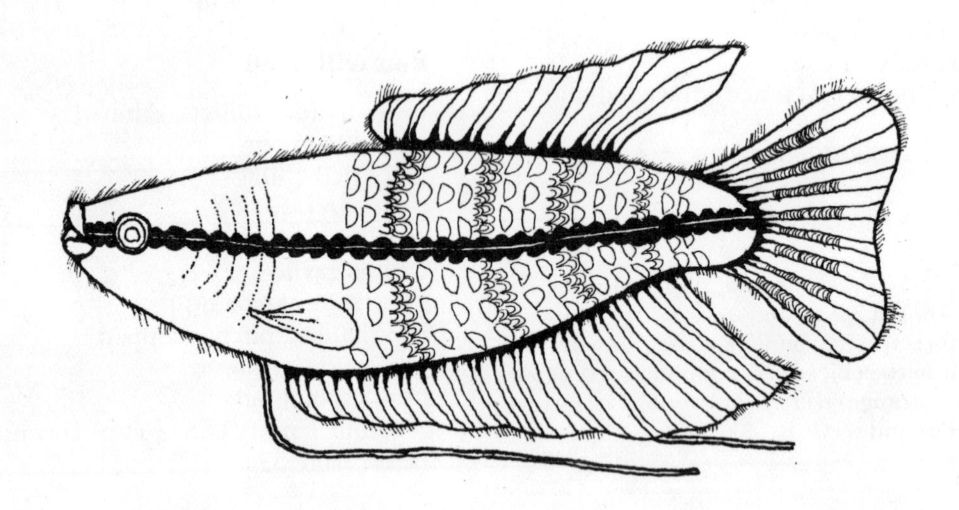

Lontong chicken (see recipe page 125)

Fish rolls (see recipe page 122)

KOREA, VIETNAM AND MACAO

Chosen, as Korea is known to the Koreans, which means the Land of Morning Calm, has been influenced in her cooking mainly by China and Japan. Throughout the Far East the Koreans are renowned as hearty eaters. Their dishes are substantial, but the number of truly Korean national dishes is not extensive. Their best known specialities are the kooks, soups of such thick consistencies that they qualify as stews.

The recipes given in this chapter are considered by the Koreans to be their most characteristic dishes.

Generous helpings of snowy rice and assorted kimchee pickles accompany all meals. The Koreans cook their rice the Chinese way.

On the other hand, the cooking of Vietnam shows mainly Chinese influence, with – in town restaurants – a French accent.

As in China, pork is the most popular meat, with poultry of all kinds being the second favourite – for those who can afford it.

Rice and vegetables form the principal diet of the people. Many of the dishes are flavoured with a salt fish sauce, a valuable source of vitamins, which most Europeans find difficult to get used to. As this relish is not readily obtainable in the West anchovy fillets, pounded to a paste, can be used as a substitute. Desserts are hardly ever served in country homes, with the exception of fruit, but sophisticated restaurants, probably as a result of French influence, present some interesting compotes.

In Macao the number of original dishes is not extensive, but Portuguese methods are often married with South Chinese ingredients. This is not surprising as Portugal first had trading centres on the island in 1559, though Macao did not become a Portuguese possession until 1887.

KOREA
GOM-GOOK
BEEF SOUP

Preparation time 10 minutes plus 30 minutes standing time
Cooking time 3 hours
To serve 4–6

You will need

2 lb. shin of beef
3½ pints (U.S. 9 cups) cold water
1 lb. young turnips, peeled
1 teaspoon black pepper
1 tablespoon light soya sauce
1 teaspoon salt
1 teaspoon finely chopped garlic
1 tablespoon ground sesame seeds
1–2 tablespoons finely chopped red pepper
1 spring onion, chopped
small pinch monosodium glutamate (optional)

Wash and dry the beef and trim off surplus fat. Place in a saucepan, cover with the water, and leave to stand for 30 minutes. Bring to the boil, skim until no more scum rises to the surface, add turnips and black pepper. Cover, reduce heat to the minimum, and simmer very gently for 2½ hours. Remove beef, cut into cubes, put into a soup tureen, sprinkle with soya sauce, salt, garlic, sesame seeds, red pepper, spring onion and monosodium glutamate. Mix well and leave to stand for 10 minutes for the spices to flavour the meat.

Keep over a pan of hot water.

Reheat the soup with the turnips, pour it over the beef and serve.

MAN-DOO
STEAMED DUMPLINGS

Preparation time 8 minutes
Cooking time 17 minutes
To serve 4–6

You will need

1 lb. uncooked, boned chicken
6 oz. bean sprouts
6 cubes bean curd
2 tablespoons lard
2 oz. peeled prawns, minced
pinch chilli powder, or more to taste
pinch monosodium glutamate (optional)
pinch freshly ground black pepper
1 tablespoon light soya sauce
1 tablespoon sesame oil
8 oz. plain flour
$\frac{1}{2}$ pint (U.S. $1\frac{1}{4}$ cups) boiling water

Mince the chicken.
Bring the bean sprouts to the boil in just enough water to cover, cook for 2 minutes, drain well and chop.
Simmer the bean curd in a little water for 2 minutes, drain and dice. Heat the lard and fry the chicken with the bean sprouts and bean curd. As soon as the chicken changes colour, add prawns, season to taste with chilli powder, monosodium glutamate, pepper and soya sauce. Sprinkle with sesame oil, stir and cook together for 1 minute. Remove from heat.
Mix the flour with the boiling water, adding the water gradually, until it forms a soft dough. Knead well, sprinkle with a little more dry flour and roll into a long sausage.
Pinch off small pieces of uniform size, and with a small rolling pin roll each piece into a 3-inch circle. Roll with quick, outward movements in such a way as to keep the centre thicker than the edges.
Put a teaspoon of the chicken filling in the middle of each circle of dough. Fold over to form a semi-circle and press the edges to seal. When all the dumplings are made, put them on a damp cloth in a steamer and steam for 10 minutes.

HO-BAE-CHOO KIM-CHEE
PICKLED CABBAGE

Follow recipe for Pickled Cucumbers (see right), using 2 lb. coarsely shredded cabbage in place of the cucumbers.

Fiery beef

MOO KIM-CHEE
PICKLED TURNIPS

Follow recipe for Pickled Cucumbers (see below) using peeled 2 lb. baby white turnips in place of the cucumber and cut into $\frac{1}{2}$-inch cubes.

OI KIM-CHEE
PICKLED CUCUMBERS

Preparation time 10 minutes plus 30 minutes standing plus 3–4 days pickling
Cooking time nil

You will need

2 lb. ridge *or* dill cucumbers
2 tablespoons salt
3 spring onions, chopped
3 cloves garlic, minced
1 teaspoon Korean dried red pepper *or* chilli
3 teaspoons finely chopped ginger
1 tablespoon light soya sauce
1 teaspoon monosodium glutamate (optional)
generous $\frac{1}{4}$ pint (U.S. $\frac{3}{4}$ cup) water

Scrub cucumbers but do not peel. Cut in half lengthways, then into $\frac{1}{2}$-inch pieces. Sprinkle with half the salt and leave to stand for 30 minutes. Rinse with cold water, drain well and dry in a clean tea towel.
Put cucumbers in a bowl, sprinkle with spring onions, garlic, red pepper, ginger, soya sauce, monosodium glutamate and the rest of the salt. Stir in the water, cover with a cloth and then a lid. Leave to pickle for 3–4 days.
Chill before serving.

BULKOKI
FIERY BEEF

(Illustrated uncooked in black and white opposite)

Preparation time 10 minutes plus 3–4 hours standing time
Cooking time 2 minutes
To serve 4

You will need

12 oz. fillet steak
1 spring onion, chopped
1 tablespoon finely chopped leek
½ shallot, finely chopped
1 clove garlic, finely chopped
¼ teaspoon sugar
½ teaspoon salt
4 tablespoons light soya sauce
1 tablespoon sesame oil
3–4 drops Tabasco
¼ pint (U.S. ⅔ cup) peanut oil

Only the best fillet steak is suitable for this dish. Cut the meat into very thin slices and beat them to flatten. Put on a dish, sprinkle with spring onion, leek, shallot, garlic, sugar, salt, soya sauce, sesame oil and Tabasco. It is the Tabasco which lends the Bulkoki its fire – the quantity can be adjusted according to taste.
Mix well and leave to stand for 3–4 hours.
Heat the peanut oil and dip in the beef slices for a few seconds. Drain and dip each piece in Bulkoki Sauce (see below) and serve at once.

BULKOKI SAUCE

Preparation time 2 minutes

You will need

¼ teaspoon salt
¼ teaspoon sugar
1 teaspoon mien chiang (Chinese bean paste)
½ teaspoon cayenne pepper
1 teaspoon sesame seeds
½ teaspoon pounded garlic
4 tablespoons soya sauce
½ teaspoon minced spring onion
1 tablespoon sesame oil

Mix all ingredients together, put in a dish and have ready on the table to dip in pieces of Bulkoki Beef as they come out of the frying pan.

SO-GO-KI TSIM
BEEF CASSEROLE, WITH SPRING ONIONS AND GREEN PEPPERS

Preparation time 10 minutes
Cooking time 4 hours
To serve 6

You will need

2 lb. stewing steak
½ pint (U.S. 1¼ cups) light soya sauce
salt
12 spring onions, chopped
4 green sweet peppers, deseeded and shredded
½ teaspoon sugar
pinch monosodium glutamate (optional)

Cut the steak into 3-inch strips. Put in a pan with the rest of the ingredients, bring to the boil, cover and simmer very slowly on lowest possible heat for 4 hours. Do not add any water but make sure that the lid of the pan fits well enough to prevent evaporation.

BAM-KYUNG-DAN
CHESTNUT DESSERT

Preparation time 12 minutes
Cooking time nil
To serve 4–6

You will need

1 lb. chestnut purée
small pinch ground ginger
¾ teaspoon ground cinnamon
2 oz. sugar
6 oz. honey
2 oz. almonds, chopped

Combine chestnut purée with ginger, cinnamon and sugar. Mix well. Taking a good teaspoon of the purée at a time, shape into small balls, dip in honey and roll in chopped almonds.

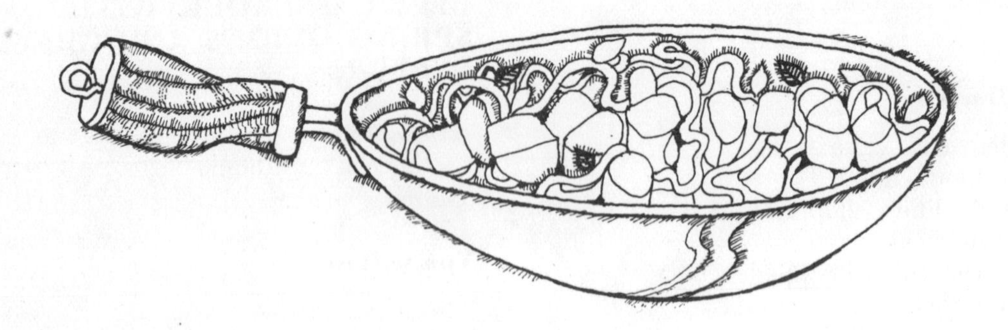

VIETNAM

NEMS
PANCAKE ROLLS

This is the Vietnamese equivalent of the Chinese spring roll – the principal difference is that pastry is used instead of batter.

Nems are delicious, stuffed with chopped, cooked meat (pork, veal, beef or chicken) mixed with lobster or crabmeat or peeled, chopped prawns. The Vietnamese are very fond of this blend of meat and shellfish – and very good it is, too.

It is usual to add to the filling some thin cooked noodles, chopped hard-boiled eggs and sliced mushrooms.

Nems should be deep-fried in hot oil, no more than three at a time, to prevent sticking, drained on kitchen paper and served piping hot. The frying takes about 10–12 minutes, when the nems should be well cooked and uniformly browned. Keep the cooked nems in a warm oven until they are all fried.

They make an excellent and substantial first course. Allow 2 nems per portion. You can vary the ingredients, depending on what you have in the larder. I don't know of many better ways of turning left-over cooked chicken into a delicious dish for 4–5 people.

Preparation time 15 minutes
Cooking time 40 minutes
To serve 4–5

You will need

8 oz. flour
salt
2 oz. butter
2 oz. cooking fat
1 large egg yolk
4 tablespoons iced water
4 oz. cooked chicken, chopped
4 oz. lobster or crabmeat, flaked (or peeled prawns, diced)
2 hard-boiled eggs, chopped
2 oz. mushrooms, chopped
4 oz. cooked noodles, chopped
freshly ground pepper
1 egg, lightly beaten
oil for deep frying

Sift the flour with a pinch of salt and rub in the fats. Blend egg yolk with the iced water and gradually mix into the dough. Knead, roll into a ball, wrap in a lightly floured cloth and leave in refrigerator until required.

Combine chicken, shellfish, hard-boiled eggs, mushrooms and noodles. Season the filling to taste with salt and pepper and mix well.

Roll out the dough very thinly, cut into 6-inch circles – the diameter of an average saucer. Put a portion of filling in a straight line across the circle, between the centre and the edge of the pastry, leaving the edges clear. Brush the edges lightly with beaten egg, fold in the sides and roll up the nem, making sure the edges are well sealed. Deep-fry, drain and serve when all are cooked.

YAM NOM GA
PRAWN AND CHICKEN SALAD
(Illustrated in black and white below)

This is a great favourite and is equally good made with pork, veal or rabbit instead of chicken.

Preparation time 10 minutes
Cooking time nil
To serve 4

You will need

8 oz. cooked chicken meat
8 oz. peeled, cooked prawns
1–2 cloves garlic, finely chopped
4 spring onions, finely chopped
$\frac{1}{4}$ teaspoon ground coriander
3 tablespoons lime *or* lemon juice
small pinch sugar
1 tablespoon vinegar
salt and pepper
small pinch chilli powder

FOR GARNISH

a few lettuce leaves, coarsely chopped
slices of lemon
8 whole prawns

Dice the chicken and 8 oz. peeled prawns. Prepare a dressing by combining the rest of the ingredients, except lettuce, lemon slices and whole prawns. Toss the chicken and prawns in the dressing and arrange on top of chopped lettuce on a serving dish. Garnish with slices of lemon and whole prawns. Serve chilled.

Prawn and chicken salad

MICHA TRONG KROEUNY
PLAICE IN FISH SAUCE

Preparation time 8 minutes
Cooking time 22–25 minutes
To serve 4

You will need

4 plaice fillets, cut into strips
2 tablespoons cornflour
peanut oil
3 spring onions, chopped
1–2 cloves garlic, finely chopped
$\frac{1}{4}$ teaspoon chilli powder
small pinch ground aniseed
$1\frac{1}{2}$ tablespoons lime *or* lemon juice
$1–1\frac{1}{2}$ teaspoons sugar
$\frac{1}{2}$ pint (U.S. $1\frac{1}{4}$ cups) light fish stock or water
$1–1\frac{1}{2}$ teaspoons Vietnamese salt fish sauce *or* 1 anchovy, pounded to a paste

Lightly dredge the fish strips with cornflour and shake off any surplus. Heat 2–3 tablespoons oil, toss the plaice strips to brown and remove from pan.

Add to the pan 2 tablespoons oil, fry spring onions for 2–3 minutes. Add garlic, chilli powder, aniseed, lime or lemon juice, sugar and stock. Bring to the boil, reduce heat and simmer for 15 minutes to concentrate the sauce.

Stir in the salt fish sauce or pounded anchovy, and cook for 1 minute. Check sauce for seasoning. Add plaice, cook for 2–3 minutes. Serve.

TUNG GOO MAN YUK
PORK WITH MUSHROOMS

(Illustrated in black and white below)

Preparation time 7 minutes
Cooking time 19–21 minutes
To serve 6

You will need

8 oz. onion, chopped
1 clove garlic, finely chopped
2–3 tablespoons oil
1 lb. lean pork, thinly sliced
4 oz. mushrooms, sliced
1 tablespoon soya sauce
small pinch monosodium glutamate (optional)
small pinch sugar
1 tablespoon brandy
generous $\frac{1}{4}$ pint (U.S. $\frac{3}{4}$ cup) stock
2 teaspoons cornflour

Fry the onion and garlic in half the oil, until soft. Add pork and fry for 3–4 minutes, stirring from time to time. Add remaining oil, heat and add mushrooms; cook for 3–4 minutes, stirring all the time. Add soya sauce, monosodium glutamate, sugar, brandy and all but 2 tablespoons of the stock. Simmer for 5 minutes.

Blend cornflour with remaining stock, add to pan and stir over a low heat until the sauce thickens. Serve with rice.

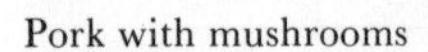

Pork with mushrooms

Fruit compote

TRY GAI
FRUIT COMPOTE
(Illustrated in black and white above)

These compotes are based on fresh, dried or canned fruits, or a mixture of all three, served in liqueur-flavoured syrup. For an authentic touch, some tropical fruit should be included in the dessert: lychees, mangoes, passion fruit, guavas, paw-paw. Grapefruit, orange and tangerine segments, sliced bananas, diced peaches, plums and pineapple are all suitable as a basis for a compote.

Preparation time 15 minutes
Cooking time 5 minutes
To serve 4

You will need

2 lb. mixed fruit, diced
water
2 oz. sugar
2–3 tablespoons liqueur
lime *or* lemon juice (optional)
ice cubes

Drain fruit of free juice, measure and make up with water to $\frac{1}{4}$ pint (U.S. $\frac{2}{3}$ cup). Put in a saucepan with the sugar and heat slowly, stirring, until sugar has dissolved.
Cook the syrup until it thickens and remove from the heat. Allow to cool and flavour with 2–3 tablespoons of liqueur of your choice. Taste the syrup and, if it is too sweet, sharpen with a little lime or lemon juice. Arrange the fruit in a compote dish, add ice cubes, pour the syrup over, chill and serve.

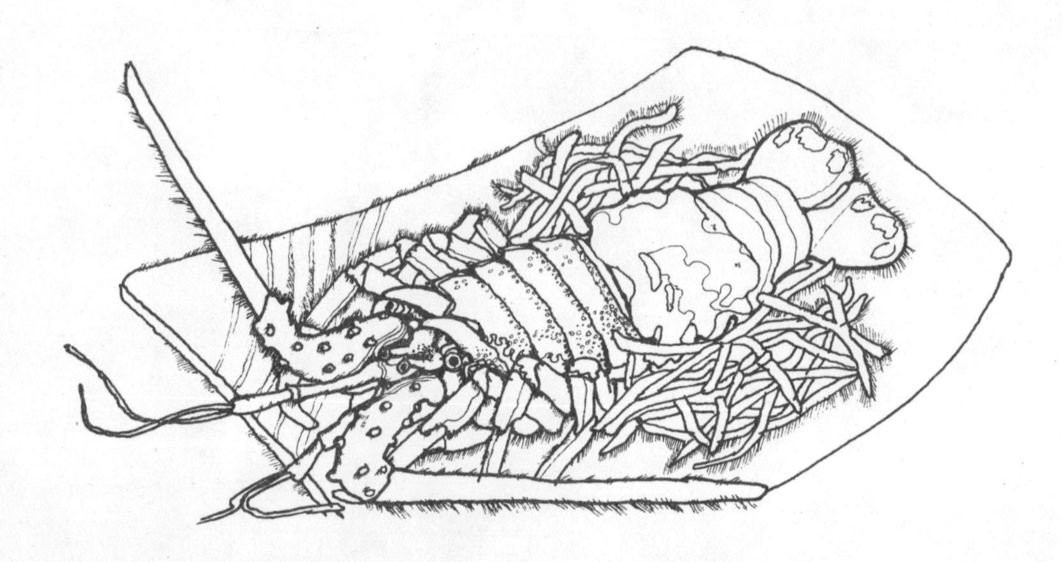

MACAO

LAGOSTA A EUGENIO DA BECA

LOBSTER EUGENIO DA BECA

Preparation time	15 minutes plus 2–3 hours to marinate
Cooking time	40–45 minutes
To serve	4

You will need

2 small live lobsters
4 oz. coconut, shredded
2 onions, chopped
1 clove garlic, chopped
$\frac{1}{4}$ pint (U.S. $\frac{2}{3}$ cup) single cream
1 teaspoon chilli powder
salt
$1\frac{1}{2}$ teaspoons paprika
$\frac{1}{2}$ teaspoon cinnamon
$\frac{1}{4}$ teaspoon nutmeg
1 teaspoon ground coriander
4 oz. butter, melted
2 tablespoons lime *or* lemon juice

Remove lobster flesh from shell and claws. Discard sac in head and black intestinal thread. Put flesh in a deep dish. Mix together the coconut, onions, garlic, cream, chilli powder, salt, paprika, cinnamon, nutmeg and coriander. Simmer carefully in a double saucepan or a bain-marie for 30 minutes; allow to cool. Then spread over the lobster and leave in a refrigerator for 2 to 3 hours.
Take the lobster out of its dressing and brush with melted butter. Grill until cooked, basting frequently with butter and the cream dressing. Arrange on a serving dish and keep hot. Gently reheat the remaining cream dressing in a bain-marie and whisk remaining melted butter into it a little at a time. Add the lime or lemon juice and serve with the lobster.

GAMBAS COM PIMENTAS
PRAWNS WITH SWEET PEPPERS

Preparation time 7 minutes
Cooking time 13–15 minutes
To serve 4

You will need

12–16 large, cooked prawns, peeled but with tails left on
salt
freshly ground black pepper
$1\frac{1}{2}$ oz. butter
2 cloves garlic, chopped
1–2 green sweet peppers, deseeded and diced
8 oz. ripe tomatoes, peeled and quartered
8 oz. stoned, ripe black olives

Season the prawns with salt and pepper. Fry in hot butter for 30 seconds on each side. Remove with a perforated spoon and keep hot.
Using the same fat, fry the garlic for 1 minute, without allowing it to brown. Add the peppers and cook, stirring, for 2–3 minutes.
Add the tomatoes, simmer for 3 minutes. Add the olives, cook for a further 5–6 minutes.
Taste, and adjust seasoning if necessary. Stir in the prawns, cook together on low heat for 1 minute and serve.

SARDINHAS EM LIMAO
SARDINES IN LEMON

Preparation time 15 minutes
Cooking time nil
To serve 4

You will need

4 large lemons
8-oz. can Portuguese sardines
salt and pepper
4 tablespoons lemon and oil dressing (see page 49)
2 hard-boiled eggs
1 teaspoon chopped parsley
bunch watercress

Wash the lemons, and cut off ends so they will stand up. Cut in half and squeeze out the juice. Remove and discard all pith. Lift the sardines out of the can, drain well, remove tails and bones and mash them. Season with salt and pepper, and sprinkle with lemon and oil dressing. Shell the eggs and chop the whites; sieve the yolks separately. Add the whites and parsley to the sardine purée and stuff the lemon cups with the mixture. Sprinkle the tops with sieved yolk. Arrange on a dish, garnish with little bunches of watercress and serve.

Note

This recipe can also be made using cooked fish, which should be flaked and bound with a little mayonnaise instead of lemon and oil dressing.

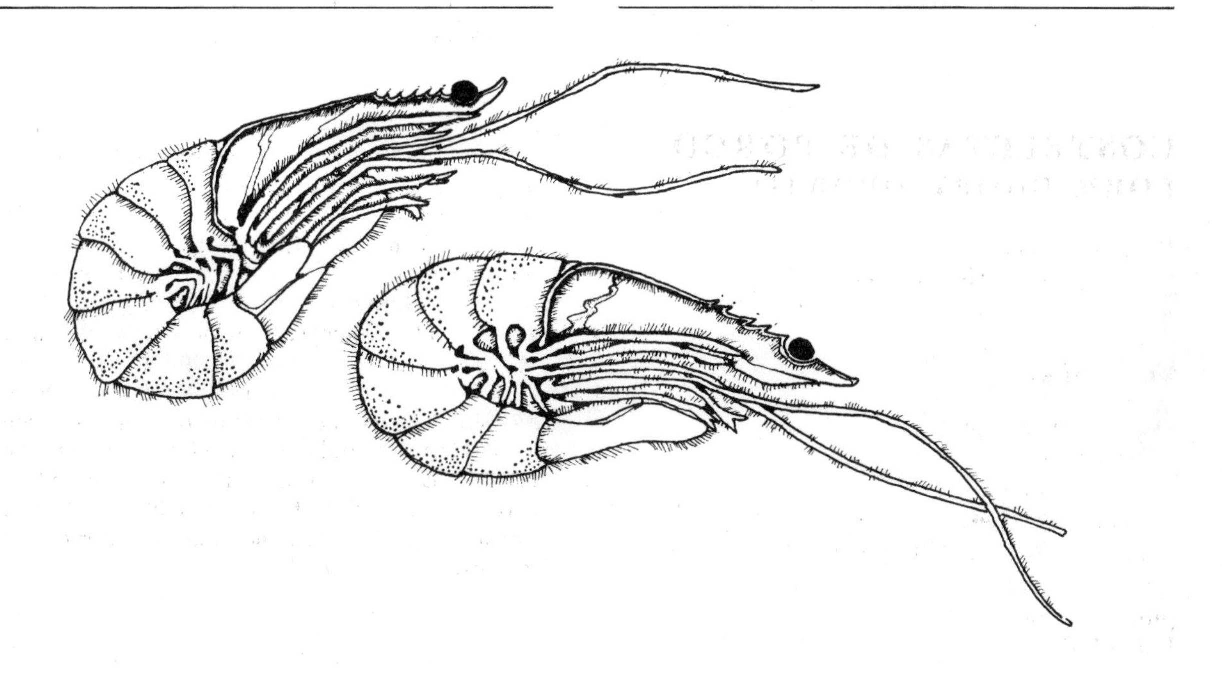

MERENGUE DE SARDINHA
SARDINE MERINGUE

Preparation time 5 minutes
Cooking time 35–40 minutes
Oven temperature 177°C., 350°F., Gas Mark 4
To serve 4

You will need

$\frac{1}{2}$ pint (U.S. $1\frac{1}{4}$ cups) white sauce (see page 59)
8-oz. can sardines
salt and pepper
3 eggs
onions cut in rings
stuffed olives

Turn on oven at temperature given above.
Make the white sauce.
Drain the sardines, remove tails and bones, mash and mix with white sauce while it is still hot. Season to taste and allow to cool. Separate the eggs and add the yolks to the mixture. Stir well and pour into a lightly buttered soufflé dish. Whisk the whites with a small pinch of salt until stiff, pile over the sardine mixture, smooth the top lightly and decorate by carefully arranging a layer of thin onion rings in whatever pattern pleases you. Put an olive, stuffed side upwards, in the centre of each onion ring, put in the preheated oven and bake for 25–30 minutes; serve immediately.

Note
This dish can be made equally successfully with any left-over cooked fish.

COSTELETAS DE PORCO
PORK CHOPS, OPORTO

Preparation time 7 minutes
Cooking time 19–23 minutes
To serve 4

You will need

olive oil for frying
4 pork chops
1 clove garlic, chopped
1 onion, chopped
4 oz. tomatoes, peeled and sliced
salt and pepper
pinch rosemary
1 small glass port

Heat a little olive oil in a frying pan and cook the chops for 3–5 minutes on each side. Remove from pan, and keep hot. Fry the garlic and onion and add the tomatoes. Season to taste with salt and pepper and sprinkle with the rosemary. Moisten with the port, cover, and simmer gently until cooked. Pour sauce over chops, and serve with boiled new potatoes and a green salad.

FRANGOS A MACAU
GRILLED CHICKEN

Preparation time 5 minutes plus 3–4 hours to marinate
Cooking time 55 minutes
To serve 4

You will need

2 poussins (young chickens)
4 oz. coconut, shredded
2 small onions, chopped
1 clove garlic, chopped
$\frac{1}{4}$ pint (U.S. $\frac{2}{3}$ cup) single cream
1 teaspoon chilli powder
$\frac{3}{4}$ teaspoon salt
$1\frac{1}{2}$ teaspoons paprika
$\frac{1}{2}$ teaspoon cinnamon
$\frac{1}{4}$ teaspoon nutmeg
1 teaspoon ground coriander
4 oz. butter, melted
2 tablespoons lime *or* lemon juice

Split each poussin in half, beat gently to flatten, put in a deep dish.
Mix coconut, onions, garlic, cream, chilli powder, salt, paprika, cinnamon, nutmeg and coriander; simmer carefully in a double saucepan, or a bain-marie for 30 minutes. Allow the mixture to cool, then spread over the chickens and leave in a refrigerator to marinate for 3–4 hours.
Take the halved chickens out of the dressing and brush with melted butter. Grill until cooked, turning to cook on both sides and basting frequently with melted butter and the cream dressing. Arrange on a serving dish and keep hot. Gently reheat the remaining cream dressing in a bain-marie. Whisk the remaining melted butter into it a little at a time; stir in the lime or lemon juice and serve with the chicken.

Wine pot in the form of the character 'fu' meaning happiness

GLOSSARY

There are few ingredients essential for preparing any of the dishes in this book that cannot be found in specialist food shops. In most cities there are shops which sell oriental foods and flavourings.

Abalone: Large shellfish, used thinly sliced and cooked for the minimum time, otherwise it becomes tough. Often available canned. Also called awabi.
Agar-agar (kanten): Gelatinous seaweed used as gelatine in hot climates because it keeps stiff at higher temperatures than gelatine.
Ajinomoto: Japanese brand name for monosodium glutamate; used for heightening flavour when cooking food.
Bamboo shoots: When not available fresh, the canned variety can be substituted.
Bean curd: See tofu.
Bean shoots: See bean sprouts.
Bean sprouts: Can be shoots or sprouts of mung peas or larger sprouts of yellow soya beans. Bought fresh or canned.
Bird's nest: Not a nest, but the gelatinous saliva of a type of swift (*Collocalia*) found on the coasts bordering the South China Sea.
Blachan: Prawn paste – substitute is anchovy paste.
Bonito shavings: Dried tunny fish used for making dashi (fish stock).
Cardamom: Aromatic spice widely used in the East to impart a pleasant flavour to curries, sweets and cakes.

Chinese cabbage: Long-leaf white or green cabbage, also called celery-cabbage. As a substitute, use Dutch white cabbage.
Chinese preserved parsnips: Obtainable from Chinese shops. Soak for 10 minutes in hot water before use.
Coriander: Spice widely used, dried, in curries. Fresh coriander leaves are used as a garnish in the Far East in the way Europeans use parsley.

Curry leaves: Leaves of a small tree or shrub (*Murraya koenigii*). The hairy, toothed leaf is pungently aromatic and often used in curries – hence its common name.
Daikon: Japanese radish, white and usually over 12 inches long. Used thinly sliced.
Dashi: Fish stock made from bonito shavings (dried tunny fish) and seaweed. See recipe page 24.
Ghee: Made from buffalo or cow butter and contains no moisture. Clarified butter can be used as an alternative. See recipe page 119.

Ginger, dried: Hot-flavoured spice used in small quantities. Powder most commonly used.
Ginger, fresh: Root has a light-brown, flaky skin; peel and shred or put through a garlic press.
Gingko nuts: Canned variety are ready for use; dried must be shelled and blanched.
Kamaboko: Japanese fish paste or fish forcemeat made into flat cakes.
Kombu: Tangle or kelp seaweed used as a flavouring in many Japanese dishes.
Lemon grass: Aromatic leaves of a plant (*Cymbopogon citratus*) cultivated in most tropical countries and used as a flavouring.
Lily petals: Chinese – soak in hot water for 15 minutes before use.
Lotus (water lily): Lotus roots are used in Chinese and Japanese dishes. Soak in hot water for 20 minutes before use. Lotus seeds if bought shelled and halved with central core removed require no further preparation unless specified in recipe.
Matsutake: Japanese tree mushroom (*Lentinus edodes*); fragrant, succulent and delicate. Found in Japanese pine forests and highly prized as a food. There are many allusions in Japanese literature and art to matsutake-gathering parties.
Mirin: Japanese wine, sweet in flavour and fortified with sake. Used for flavouring soups and sauces. Sweet white wine or sherry may be used as a substitute.
Miso: Fermented soya bean paste with added salt and malt. Used in Japanese soups.
Monosodium glutamate: Flavouring or seasoning powder used in Japanese and Chinese cooking. It is a white crystalline substance made from grains and vegetables, which is supposed to enhance the flavour of food without having much flavour of its own. Should be used very sparingly. If quantities of ingredients in recipe are increased do not increase amount of monosodium glutamate. Sold pure or mixed with other flavourings such as salt under a number of brand names such as Ajinomoto, Ve-tsin, Accent and Aromat.

Mushrooms, dried: There are a number of varieties. All should be soaked before use.
Nori: Purple laver seaweed with a fishy flavour. Sold dried in black sheets or squares. It is heated to crisp it, then crushed and sprinkled over food. Also used for wrapping round vinegared rice cakes or sushi. See recipe page 16.
Oyster sauce: Strained concentrate of oysters cooked in soya sauce and salt water. Used in cooking to heighten flavour of food.
Persimmon: Date plum, joint of Japanese origin. When ripe, resembles a tomato in shape, size and colour.
Poppy seeds: Not only used for flavouring in Malaysia but also for thickening gravies. Do not substitute flour or cornflour but use ground peanuts or cashew nuts instead.
Prawn crackers: Far Eastern equivalent of European potato crisps. See recipe on page 83.
Saffron: Dried stigmas of *Crocus sativus*. Used for colouring and flavouring rice. Very expensive as yield per plant is small.

Sake: Japanese wine brewed from rice. About the same strength as sherry which may be used as a substitute in cooking. For drinking purposes it is served in small quantities, usually warmed, though in hot weather it is often served chilled.
Shoyu: Japanese for soya sauce.
Soya bean: Valuable source of protein in the Far East where other protein food such as meat is too expensive for many people to eat at every meal.
Soya sauce: Also called soya bean sauce or soya and in America, soy, is made from soya bean, grain malt, yeast and salt. The light variety is generally used for cooking and the dark for table use.
Tamarind: Fruit of the tamarind tree. The pods are filled with an acid, juicy pulp. In many Asian countries tamarind juice is used in preference to vinegar or lemon juice. For cooking purposes, use dried tamarind. Soak it in a little water, remove fibres, strain the juice through muslin and use as directed. For 1 oz. tamarind allow 5 tablespoons water. When using tamarind for a sweet and sour sauce, add sugar to taste, heat to dissolve and mix well. Tamarind juice should be used for dishes intended for eating the same day. As a substitute, use lime or lemon juice or vinegar – in that order.
Taro: Starchy root of a tuber of the arum family, much liked in Japan. When not available, potatoes may be used instead.
Tofu: Bean curd. It is unique in many important respects. It costs very little, it is one of the cheapest foods, yet can easily be made into a great delicacy. Famous in China for thousands of years, served in the humblest homes and at the most sumptuous of banquets, it is a valuable source of proteins, calcium, phosphorus and iron. Whilst defying comparison with any other food, tofu blends with all foods and can be boiled, fried, steamed or eaten with rice or salad. It can be cooked with meat, fish or vegetables and is excellent for thickening soups, giving them body without stodge.
Toso: Very special kind of sake, made to a secret formula, served on ceremonial occasions. It has been made in Japan for over a thousand years – as far back as the Heian period (794–1185 A.D.) and is reputed to have inspired the splendid outcrop of drinking songs which still survive in the folklore of the nation.
Turmeric: Orange-yellow coloured rhizomes, widely used to flavour and colour food. Only a small quantity is needed, no more than $\frac{1}{2}$ teaspoon for a dish for 4 people. Often used as a substitute for the much more expensive saffron.

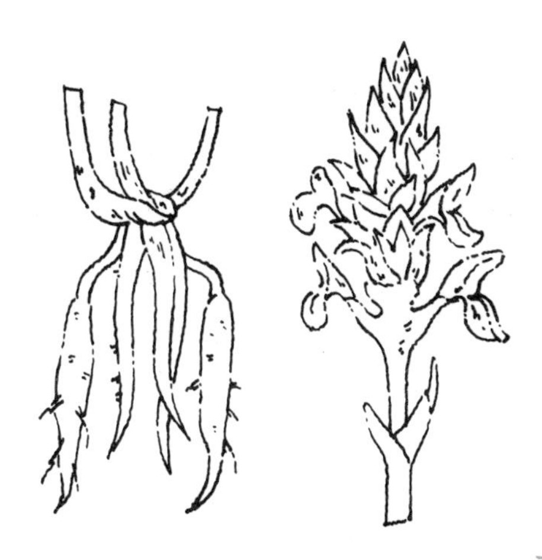

Ve-tsin: See monosodium glutamate.
Water chestnut: Bulb of Asian marsh plant. Used as a vegetable. When fresh must be washed and peeled. Canned it is ready for use.
Water-chestnut flour: Dried water chestnut ground to a flour; in China used as a thickener, binder and batter ingredient.

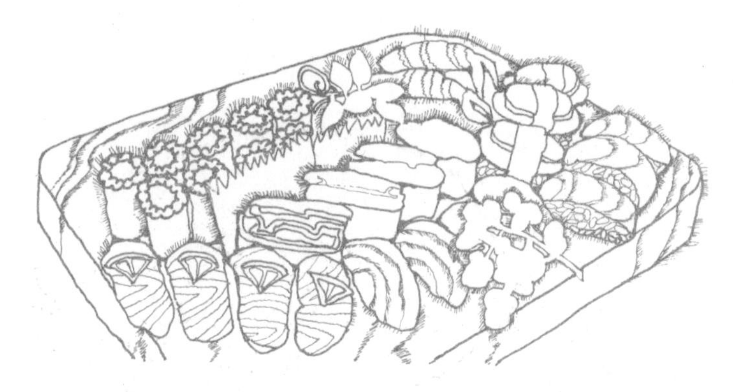

INDEX

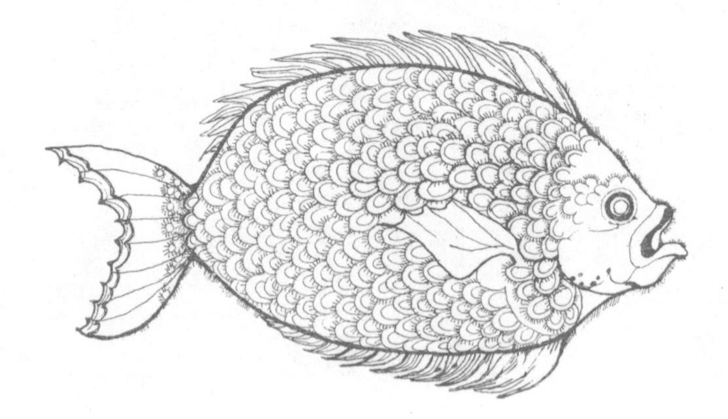

SPIC
ALLSP
CHILLI

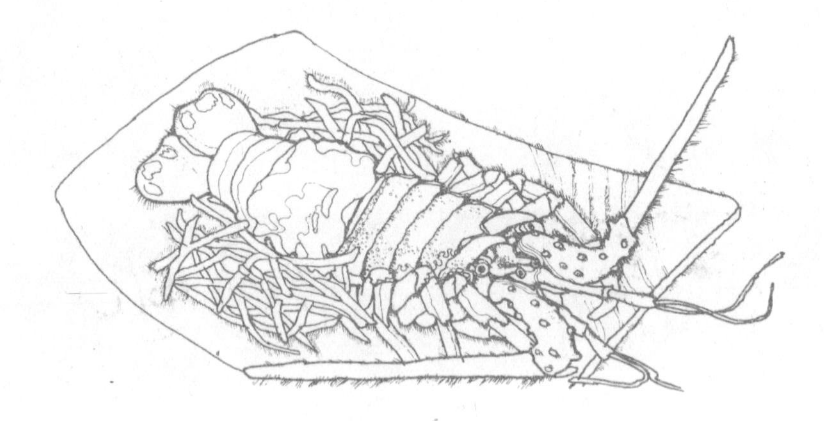

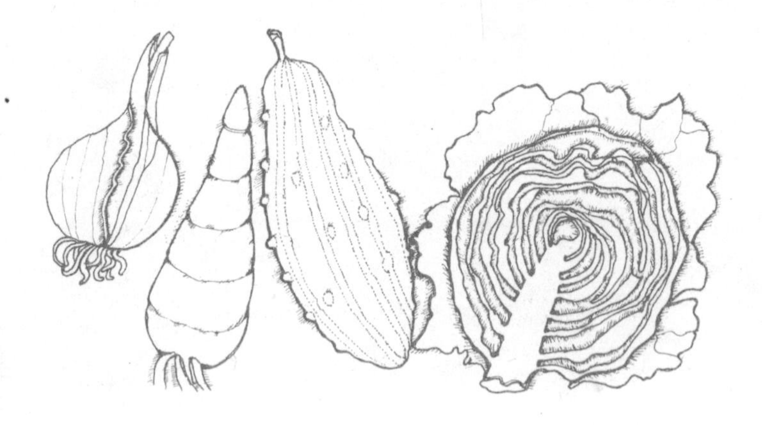

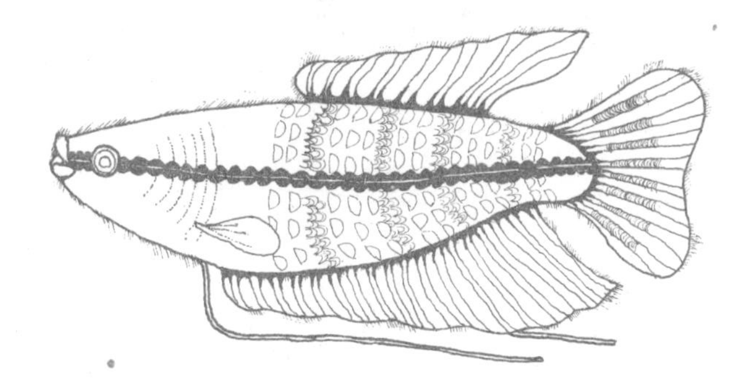

ACKNOWLEDGEMENTS

The author and publisher thank the following for their co-operation in supplying photographs for this book

For colour photographs

AUSTRALIAN RECIPE SERVICE
Chicken with peaches and almonds *page 90*
Ginger pears with lychees

FRUIT PRODUCERS' COUNCIL
Front cover; Apple and mint sambal, Mixed fruit sambal, Duck with pineapple, Satay, Chicken curry, Sashimi, in the form of a Japanese garden which was created by Mr. Igarashi of the Hiroko restaurant, London

For black and white photographs

ASIA MAGAZINE
Deep-fried prawns and vegetables *page 32*
Stuffed pancakes with palm hearts *page 71*
Curried chicken salad *page 125*
Fiery beef *page 130*

AUSTRALIAN RECIPE SERVICE
Sweet and sour lobster with pineapple *page 92*
Chicken with peaches and almonds *page 98*

HERRING INDUSTRY BUREAU
Fresh fish *page 23*

NEW ZEALAND LAMB INFORMATION BUREAU
Grilled lamb chops *page 36*
Lamb vindaloo *page 60*

NORWEGIAN PRAWN INDUSTRY
Prawn and chicken salad *page 133*

SUTTON & SONS LTD.
Dwarf French beans *page 16*

VICTORIA AND ALBERT MUSEUM
Wine pot *page 139*

WHITE FISH AUTHORITY
Sole with bananas *page 72*
Fish in coconut milk *page 123*

YOUNG'S SEAFOODS
Sweet and sour prawns *page 19*
Prawns with peppers and pineapple *page 94*

The author and publisher also thank the following for assistance with the phonetic spelling of the dishes of their countries

Embassy of the Republic of Indonesia, London
Korean Embassy, London
Office of the High Commissioner for Malaysia, London
Embassy of the Republic of the Philippines, London
Casa de Portugal, London
Information Service of Thailand, London

and the following restaurants in Singapore where many of the dishes illustrated were cooked and photographed
The Korean (Korea)
Robinson's (China)
Fujiya (Japan)
The Cockpit (Indonesia)
Lontong House (Malayasia and Singapore)

China
The Far East
Hong
Thailand
Malaya
Singapore
Indonesi